Grand Wishes

Advocating to Preserve the Grandparent-Grandchild Bond

Susan Hoffman

Collegare Press

Collegare Press
PO Box 5622
Newport Beach, CA 92662

ISBN 13 978-0-9799168-0-9

Cover design: Nita Gilson, Gilson Graphics

Interior design: Gwen Gades, Purple Penguin Press

Third Printing 2016

Grand Wishes

This book is dedicated to Jacob,
who lives within my heart and because of
him I began a new journey.

Acknowledgements

Marchelle Hammack: my most constructive critic, diligent coach and enthusiastic supporter. I am so grateful that we connected. I humbly thank you for your proofreading, editing and creative additions.

Arnold Schwarzenegger: Without your golden signature there would be no progress: thank you for your support of my bill. Thank You for caring about grandparents.

Assemblyman Van Tran: You opened the door: Thank you for believing in me and trusting me to work in a proactive role along side your legislative team.

Dr. Lillian Carson: You are a pillar of wisdom: Thank you for your endless patience and for always being there for me to lean on.

Disenfranchised Grandparents: Thank you for sharing your stories and supporting one another. I appreciate your confidence in my organization and commend you on your courage to participate.

Sheryl Edgar, Esq.: You may have created a monster: Thank you for suggesting the idea of empowerment and thinking far outside the box.

Rick Harrison, M.A. MFT: Infinite possibilities and opportunities: Thank you for the numerous and clever Rickisms that have cued me to remember to stay on track on my path to peace.

Contents

They say genes skip
generations.

Maybe
That's why grandparents
Find their grandchildren

So likable. ~joan mcintosh

Introduction

Watermarks dot the pages of my journal. These are my tears. It is not so much the content that makes me sad; in fact writing about my feelings lightens me. The grief stems from the constraints I live with that keep me from my grandson. Journaling is the one way I can share my life with my only grandson.

I learned about the meaning of disenfranchised grandparents by living through it, a dilemma that is more prevalent than I had previously thought. Sadly, there are many other grandparents that share my fate. Our beloved grandchildren live only within our hearts and are no longer a part of our physical presence. We share our pain, via e-mail, phone and meetings, to connect with one another and proclaim that this travesty no longer needs to be hidden. Society should know about this legal and personal limbo in which so many grandparents find themselves. Society also needs to be concerned about a child's right to emotional well being and how this is threatened when attachments are broken.

Denied visitation between grandparents and grandchildren is often brought about because of a disconnection and breakdown within an extended family. It doesn't take much for this to occur, often with no warning or explanation. There is always the possibility of a family feud or rift, however, mostly it is a case of esoteric discontent on behalf of the parent(s) toward the grandparent[s], and it is almost always a control issue. Throughout the Internet there are a multitude of grandparent and children's rights organizations to be found. There are scores of message boards, blogs, telephone and e-mail support, research studies, educational articles from psychologists and attorneys, and a multitude of attorney referrals. The numerous resources prove the need for public policy programs and private organizations to address this problem.

Examples of painful true stories are endless and the range of excuses the grandparents were given from the parents, if any, were mixed and none made the case for complete elimination of grandparents from the grandchildren's lives, barring extreme behavioral circumstances [criminal, deviant, danger]. The parents, in most cases, chose to remove the person, rather than the problem.

The idea of "grandparenthood" has always been a natural progression from parenthood, a role that traditionally holds honor and respect. Today, it seems that grandparents are no longer so "grand." Denied access can happen to any grandparent, no one is exempt. It crosses the socio-economic strata and all boundaries. We never think it could happen to us; I certainly didn't.

I now find myself in the role of advocate and activist for grandparents' and children's rights. There is something surreal about the idea of fighting for a child just so he or she can be loved by someone. Is there truly a limit on how many people a child is allowed to have in their lives who will love him or her? I believe that children can't have too many caring adults who love them; how fortunate for them when they have them, and even more so when they get to keep them.

My purpose is to raise awareness and provide useful information to those grandparents experiencing denied visitation. I invite each reader to begin taking action, for themselves and their grandchildren, or perhaps for others in need because everyone can make a difference.

The intent for this book is to offer up the idea to grandparents and others that it is both worthwhile and necessary to become involved in the pursuit of preserving family values, specifically the extended family. No grandparent should ever lose a moment's time that could be spent with a grandchild and no child should lose precious moments with a loving grandparent. All grandparents must unite and take back power for themselves and the child. Preserve it. Protect it. Embrace it. It could happen to anyone. It could happen to you.

This isn't a debate between grandparents' rights and parents' rights; it's about serving the best interests of children, by allowing them to maintain vital connections with grandparents [and significant others] with whom they have formed an attachment and developed a relationship. A child's emotional welfare is at stake. The child loses an entire side of his or her kinship system when grandparents are removed; access to practical, financial and emotional resources are eliminated as well. In many cases the child will never know the other half of his or her family.

My observation is that no matter what is going on

between parent and grandparents, the children MUST come first. My desire is to see children stop being treated as property.

Topics covered in this book describe the genesis of the support group and non-profit organization I created, Advocates For Grandparent Grandchild Connection [website: www.grandparentchildconnect.org], personal interviews and articles honoring the importance of the role of grandparents, examples of the effects on children and grandparents when the bond is broken, a collection of grandparent stories, my experience of my quest to pass Bill AB2517, allowing grandparents to petition the court for grandchild visitation, which was enacted into law by the California Assembly and Legislature on January 1, 2007, and a discussion about the meaning of grandparents rights.

If you're not a grandparent now, you may be someday. Think back on your relationship with your grandparents. Chances are there was, or is, some connection there that gives meaning to your life today.

"Surely two of the most satisfying experiences in life must be those of being a grandchild or a grandparent."
Donald A. Norberg

The reason Grandchildren
and Grandparents
get along so well
is that they have
a common enemy

~sam levenson

One

The Alienation Of Grandma: The Lost Connection

Once I was a grandmother, but I was stripped of that title and all it means by circumstances beyond my control. I was forbidden to see my only grandson ever again by his biological mother and adoptive father. This occurred when Jacob was five years old. My son, the biological father, and Jacob's mother never married. They loved each other once but their relationship changed. They became estranged and my son eventually gave up all rights to his son.

Given these circumstances, which were awkward and sometimes difficult, Jacob and I still managed to continue our relationship. I loved Jacob even before I met him. He is, after all, a part of me. Jacob's mother and I got along well enough for her to trust me to baby sit and be a part of their lives. She was comfortable with me to the point of seeking my assistance emotionally and physically. I established my role as a grandparent and was able to see Jacob regularly, to hold him, to care for him, to play with him, to enjoy him. What fun we had! I was Grandma Susan. When Jacob's mother eventually married another man, my regular visits with my grandson became less frequent until they were eventually non-existent, at which point the court's involvement became necessary. Jacob's mother felt it was in his best interest for the new stepfather to legally adopt him, and therefore, her campaign began for the cooperation of my son and myself to allow the newly formed family to form an "intact" status. The parents both promised me that my relationship with the child I loved so much would remain the same. I trusted them. But on the very day of the adoption, Jacob's mother and now legal father sent a letter that stated that they no longer wanted me in Jacob's life, terminating my visits.

I felt betrayed. I believed that they would keep their word and honor their agreement. I was wrong. I kept replaying in my head the sequence of events as I struggled to make some sense of the new situation. Can't they see how Jacob interacts with me when we are together? Isn't our mutual affection obvious? What about his feelings? His heartbreak when he realizes there is no more Grandma Susan? Will he think I've abandoned him? They didn't explain why they were pushing me out of Jacob's life. Legally, they didn't have to. It's the law, the attorneys told me. "When a stepparent adopts their stepchild they assume all the duties of parenthood as well as all of the parental rights. Those parental rights include the right to decide who may or may not visit the minor child." The circumstances changed in the eyes of the law because, now the family was "intact," and when this occurs, in most states, grandparents have no right to petition the court for visitation, especially when both parents agree to the denial, reasonable or not. Three and a half years went by. I felt powerless to bring Jacob back into my life. He would outgrow the toys I kept for him. The games we played would go untouched. The tires would soon go flat on his little blue bike and the training wheels would never be removed. It seemed there would be no more shared experiences with Grandma Susan. When Jacob was eight years old, a window of opportunity opened; his parents separated and to my surprise, the adoptive dad contacted me and invited me back into Jacob's life. He claimed that he was now the recipient of Jacob's mother's wrath and vindictiveness and he now empathized with me. He apologized to me. Jacob and I reunited with ease, nearly picking up where we had left off. It was a dream come true, and every minute we had together was cherished. There was bike riding, movie watching, laughter, hugs, kisses, some card playing, eating out, eating in, beach going, homework helping, sketchbook time and just being close with one another. The window abruptly closed after just four months. Jacob's mother appeared to be threatened by our visits and the idea of not having total control over Jacob enraged her. Even though his adoptive father seemingly had good intentions, the effort to take a stand against Jacob's mother required a tremendous amount of strength and courage, and the price, ultimately, became too high for him to continue to fight. Sadly, Jacob is the one who ends up paying the price of parental inconsistency.

I am still a grandmother, if only in my eyes and in my heart. I think Jacob also believes this now that he is older and able to process more. For now, I cannot be apart of his life: sharing his triumphs, his disappointments or providing any wisdom I might share. I will miss hearing him say, "I love you." Or saying those words to him. Regardless, I continue to love him always. Daily. I carry him with me wherever I go, I think of him every day. My heart is broken. This can happen to anyone.

Everyone
needs to have
access both to
grandparents
and
grandchildren in
order to be a full human being.

~margaret mead

Two

Upon Becoming An Activist: Empowered Boomers

"Does anyone here have trouble sleeping?" asked Brenda. We all raised our hands.

We could be considered a unique group: grandparents who are orphaned in a sense because we have lost contact with our grandchildren. So, once a month we gather together in a community center in Corona Del Mar California to share our stories and lend support to one another as a way of coping with our grief as well as reaching out to assist one another. During a recent meeting, someone brought up the issue of disturbed sleep; it turns out it is one of the side-effects of the frustration and emptiness we all experience that at times threatens our emotional stability and often disrupts our nocturnal rest. When sleep does occur, it can sometimes provide a pleasant opportunity to visit those lost grandchildren through the wonderwork of dreams.

The support group was conceived by me out of desire to connect with other grandparents who were experiencing visitation issues with their grandchildren. Up until then, my only connection with grandparents in similar situations was through e-mail and telephone, since most were scattered across the country. I wanted face to face interaction, but there were no groups in Orange County specifically dedicated to grandparents who have been denied visitation. So I placed an ad in a local newsletter, calling the group, "Lost Access." The Laguna Beach Senior/Community Center gave us a room, and we had our first meeting. We were a small intimate group in the beginning, no more than five at each gathering. It has been less than two years since that first meeting, and although we remain small, the interest is growing as we continue to receive newcomers, and consistently see familiar faces. The focus of the group, besides support, is child advocacy and activism in order to secure our rights to sustaining attachments with our grandchildren. The most popular statement from newcomers seems to be, I thought I was the only one that this was happening to. Grandparents are so grateful to learn that they are not alone, and that there is empathy and even solutions in some cases, as simple as continuing to send gifts and cards even if they are not acknowledged. The group forum provides a safe environment in which to commiserate when necessary, and exchange ideas and information.

My perception of the individuals that attend is that they are energetic, focused, intelligent, loving grandparents, mostly baby boomers, who previously had a strong bond and ongoing relationship with their grandchildren, and are dumbfounded when denied access by their own children. There is embarrassment and humiliation about their grown children's behavior. Often, they blame themselves in some way for mistakes in their child's upbringing, as a way of making sense of the sudden rejection. The truth is, parental influence is a part not the whole; as the saying goes, " parents can't take credit for all their children's successes. Neither can they assume responsibility for the failures."

Proudly, I see an ongoing camaraderie developing with each get-together, as we have grown to look forward to spending time with one another; the sharing and listening has developed into mutual concern and the healing has become a journey of personal growth. A guest speaker, Rick Harrison, M.A. MFT, once praised us. "You could all be doing something else today, yet here you are, choosing to do the work."

It was through the group's encouragement that I continued to pursue grandparent legislation and concurrently establish an organization. Getting a bill passed and getting approved by the IRS as a non-profit both proved to be challenging endeavors. The legislative activity was such an interesting and educational challenge for me, and despite all my naiveté, everything fell into place with very few problems. The tedious non-profit application process became a lesson in patience and perseverance; non-profit status was granted by a letter of approval, a huge cause for celebration.

The organization first grew out of association with a website called Grandparents-R-Us, created by a friend, Mary Frasier, who kindly gave me a page on her website. On this page I expressed my concern for the growing problem of denied grandparent visitation and offered support and information on the website. I began receiving calls and emails from distraught grandparents from around the country. An independent and separate entity devoted specifically to one issue was created, Advocates For Grandparent Grandchild Connection, therefore this is the name in which the non-profit operates, and also serves as the foundation for our group, Lost Access. The organization has the power through Internet exposure to serve a larger national network, while the individual group[s] provide a source of community outreach. The organization provides counseling, education, resource information, referrals, proposes legislation and continues to build an outreach program.

The calls and emails continue to come in at a steady pace. Most of the calls are from local Orange County residents who are looking for answers and support from someone who understands because they have had a similar experience. Many of the ones that call end up attending the meetings. The emails are mostly from grandparents who live out of the area and out of state. It also must be noted, the problem crosses all socio-economic and cultural boundaries, no one is exempt. Again, just hearing back from someone who understands goes a long way toward the healing process. Taking the time to answer questions and provide information, such as links to state statutes or attorney referrals, is always met with notes of appreciation. Talking about the problem is the first step, and providing a safe environment in which to do so builds trust and opens the door to recovery and problem solving.

The purpose is summarized best in the "Mission" statement:

> *Advocates For Grandparent Grandchild Connection was created on behalf of the children who have been denied access to their grandparents. It*

is comprised of grandparents, grandchildren, and parents united for the purpose to advocate for those children, to educate and bring awareness, and support the grandparents, who suffer from the loss of affection and contact with their grandchildren. We are a non-profit 501 [c][3] organization.

You

Do not

Really understand

Something unless

You

Can explain it to your

Grandmother

~proverb

Three

Importance Of Grandparents: The Vital Connection

Much has been written in the last decade about the role grandparents play in the lives of families. There seems to be an influx of books and websites that reinforce the vital importance of grandparents and the reason for this trend is twofold: the role's stature, as of late, has been threatened, and the increase of boomer grandparents has put a spotlight on this issue. The word, "grand-Parent" in itself, describes that essential part of a family structure, second only to parents. Grandparents are so important that often, today's grandparents are becoming the primary caregivers to their grandchildren, approximately 6 million in the United States. Whether raising grandchildren or not, grandparents are often regarded with affection, remembered with fond memories and are a powerful influence in grandchildren's lives. They are caregivers, playmates, confidants, helpers, a support system and connection to the past and the extended family. "Every child needs an older person to be crazy about," is a profound observation by Dr. Arthur Kornhaber, Ph. D, and one I most definitely agree with.

Upon Loving My Grandparents

I grew up with the benefit of knowing my grandparents, all four of them. I was crazy about them, and I had the comfort of knowing they were even crazier about me. I always felt the unconditional love that was special and unique and more precious than any other, because it was optional, without the rules and pressures of parenthood. I felt a different kind of closeness to my grandparents than to my parents. They were a big part of my life, and I am grateful that I had most of them well into my adulthood. The bond was formed early on, and provided me with a sense of security and stability. All four of them were actively involved with me and interested in my life. I believe this helped give me a strong foundation, and I credit them for their contribution to my childrearing. I always felt that I could depend on them and I always felt loved. It was reciprocal; I wanted them in my life just as much as they wanted me in theirs. Once, during a turbulent time, following some sort of feud, my maternal grandmother was banished from our household, along with all contact, and missing her so much, I put myself in jeopardy to see her on the sly. The everlasting bond was invincible against threat.

My paternal grandparents lived long enough to become active great-grandparents to my children. They are the only ones that I trusted enough to leave my children with overnight.

Each one of my grandparents had a different and

unique way of grand-parenting, but one constant is they all spent time with me. They didn't have to, but they did it because they wanted to.

Coy, my maternal grandfather, was the one I was closest to, and sadly, the one I had the least time with. He was actually a step-grandparent because we weren't blood related, but that was just a technicality. He was more like a big best friend. I went everywhere with him; I was a part of his world. We did everything together; we had a Saturday night ritual: eating apples followed by chocolate chip ice cream as we watched Roller Derby and Gunsmoke on TV. We had an ongoing game of opening and closing the doors to the TV cabinet; I closed them during his programs, and [pre-remote] he had to get up each time and re-open them. This playful test of wills went on until the rolled up newspaper appeared; he used to scare me by snapping it across his hand until it shredded into pieces. Eventually, either he ended up foregoing the program and playing with me or I gave in and watched his program with him. Either way we had a good laugh.

My grandmother, Blanche, was a workaholic, somewhat detached and rather vain, preferring not to be called "grandma," so I ended up calling both my grandparents by their first names. In reality, they probably treated me more like a little adult. They even took me to work with them; they owned a dry cleaners in Los Angeles. Blanche loved hamburgers, so we always stopped off on the way home at a drive-in, possibly an original McDonalds, car tray and all. Blanche was an expert seamstress and delighted in making all of my clothes; she would dress me up and proudly show me off to everyone. Whenever they took time off for vacation road trips, I went along, always standing on the front seat of the white Chevy station wagon, in between them. We were a family in the true sense; I was the light of their lives and I knew it.

The best thing that came from my parents' marriage, and divorce, was my paternal grandparents, whom I didn't call by first names. My dad's sister, my aunt, once described to me how my grandparents felt about me: "They think the sun rises and sets by you." I never forgot her statement, and looking back, I felt that from them. Jessie, my grandmother, was often my caregiver while my mother worked; so much of my early years were spent in her presence. My fondest memories of her are when I became an adult and voluntarily spent time with her. It was during that time that I gained respect for the job of homemaker, a role she excelled at. She seemed to know how to do everything, and did it well, probably perfectly. She ran a tight ship. There was no fudging on chores; they were done the right way or not at all. She patiently taught me how to cook, from scratch, with "do-overs" until it was correct. She could make anything, and sometimes even something out of nothing, and it always turned out tasting wonderful. She was a role model: for honesty, integrity, diligence and perseverance. She was a benevolent taskmaster.

Grandpa Louie was fun loving and playful, kind to all children, grandchildren included. He spent hours and hours telling stories and having conversations with me and then with my own children, always giving us his undivided attention. He gave us the best gift of all, time. While Grandma and I were cooking in the kitchen, Grandpa could be found tossing the ball back and forth, to my then toddler son, patiently, tirelessly, for what seemed like hours. What I wouldn't give to have one more cooking lesson, and look out the window over the clothes line and hear the laughter as they played one more game of catch.

My children come from what I call the "me-ish" generation; they are more focused on themselves and less family-oriented. They are less involved with grandparents and visits are few and far between. Given the characteristics of the nuclear generation they occupy, they remain respectful and hopefully, realize how vital grandparents are even in adulthood. For my son, a pivotal moment was seeing my mother's face light up when he walked into her hospital room. He later explained that he kept seeing her face the rest of the day, following the visit, and how happy she was to see him, and that perhaps a "goodnight" call from him would mean a lot.

In this example, the connection has always been there, but it may not always be visible. In my children's situation, they spent a lot of time around their grandmother when they were young, but not so much as adults, yet the bond remains.

On being a grandparent, my experience may be less conventional and more spiritual in nature, as I no longer have physical contact, and my actual time spent was limited, before my role was cut short. I would have to say that during the five years and four months that I enjoyed interacting with my grandson, I was hands-on and modeled the more playful rough and tumble persona, modeling both my grandfathers.

We played Candyland, Hungry Hippo, Legos, and concocted various silly scenarios with action figures. We spent hours playing street hockey, where the joke was always on me as I was always the one who crawled under every car on the street retrieving the puck. We had a try at baseball; I was the pitcher. And I once bought him a child-size plastic starter set of golf clubs. My fondest recollection of our time spent together was when he was eight and we discovered that we each had a love of drawing. The two of us sat side-by-side on the sofa in relative silence, each with a sketch pad, completely losing track of time. When it was time for me to go he would beg, "aaw, don't go yet." I like to think he inherited his affinity for drawing from me. Our shared love of art and drawing together, linked us, as we concentrated with undivided attention, sitting next to one another; this mutual affection and comfort with each other reinforcing the importance of having a grandparent-grandchild relationship.

Extreme and toxic circumstances aside, grandparents should remain an integral part of a child's life. Whatever differences occur within families or between parent and grandparent, they should be set aside for the sake of the child.

Balboa Island:

John Scudder Remembers His Grandmother, April 22, 2007

It was Sunday afternoon during the springtime when I met with my dear friend, John Scudder, to talk about the importance and "grandness" of grandparents, a subject near and dear to his heart and one we have explored many times before.

We settled into the oversized Adirondack chairs on the wood deck situated under the massive coral tree that consumes most of John's yard. It was the calm before the rain; the air was still and the clouds lightly frosted the pale sky like spun cotton candy, creating a soft blanket of quiet for ease of conversation. The house is vintage Balboa Island, well cared for and restored to maintain the original architecture. It sits on a corner lot on the north bay front, just steps to the harbor, with sweeping views of the mainland. This is the house that belonged to John's beloved grandmother, Laura Scudder, a fitting place to reflect the importance of grandparents.

John loved his grandmother so much that he made the ultimate tribute; he bought her house so he could live in it. He is in the process of designing a sort of museum room in a former downstairs bedroom so that he may display his collection of "Laura Scudder" memorabilia. I got a sneak preview of some of the collectibles that fill overhead shelves and nostalgic black and white glossy photos strewn across the antique roll top desk.

As the family historian, John is constantly on the lookout for Laura Scudder memorabilia, forever searching Internet sites for items. In this same month a public television station recently aired the documentary that John produced some eighteen years ago, titled, "Laura," chronicling her life.

John began with a fond memory that has remained with him. He told me he was about ten years old and he had gone to work at the plant that day with his dad. He had just got his first wallet, which was a big deal for a little boy because it was a future step toward manhood. John decided he wanted to take his grandmother, whom he called "Madre" out to lunch with the five dollars he had in his new wallet. Once they entered the restaurant and were seated at a table for two, John became concerned that the five dollars wouldn't go very far. John said, "It was a swanky restaurant, with long menus and a maitre'd."After perusing the menu, he told me his grandmother asked, "Johnny, what are you going to have?" He replied, "A hamburger," the least expensive item on the menu. Madre's response, "That's what I'll have too."

"She was sweet to let me enjoy my dignity," John explained.

When asked, John continued to summarize his feelings about his relationship with his grandmother. He told me that the fondness he had as a child is the same that he has today. "I appreciate now how much time she spent with me. I felt important and always felt her strength, and all the little courtesies, that I wouldn't learn to appreciate for years."

John always knew that there was plenty of love to go around; she loved her role of grandmother and that of a working woman.

John concluded, "I am so grateful for her, and think of her with fondness, reverence and most of all appreciation. Did you notice, I'm speaking of her today fifty years later!"

MONTECITO:

Dr. Lillian Carson, Ph. D, author of *The Essential Grandparent,* May 20, 2007

This time my interview took me about 140 miles out of town to a Santa Barbara community called Montecito, California where Dr. Lillian Carson lives. I consider Lillian not only an expert about the role of grandparenting, but a mentor and friend. Up until now our communication over the last four years had been through e-mails and telephone calls. She has consistently remained a source of support and information about grandparent issues and someone I find easy to connect with, sharing similar views on this subject.

Once settled into my hotel, I felt the need to walk off the stiffness from a 2 ½ hour car ride. I strode off toward the pedestrian friendly trail that runs along the Santa Barbara harbor. Refreshed from the brisk salt air, I was ready to navigate the four short miles to the Montecito village where I had an invitation to dinner in her home.

Lillian and her husband, Sam, greeted me warmly as I

stepped into their quiet hideaway tucked from public view with a shield of lush vegetation. The house is an architectural delight, and why wouldn't it be, Sam is a distinguished architect by profession and Lillian a collector of art. The house was indeed a treat to experience. The furniture held true to the integrity of the home design because each piece was an object of art, designed by an architect, reminding me of the classics I once studied in a contemporary art history class years before.

Lillian and I settled into the living room for my interview, a room that challenged my concentration with so much to visually explore; I kept diverting my attention to the massive glass doors where just outside grew lush mondo grass and exotic bamboo, providing a serene wall of privacy. I admit I was fascinated with the unique appearance of the lumpy grass. Back to business.

I asked Lillian about the inception of her journey into the nuances of grandparenthood, the development of a website and the publishing of a book. Her first statement, "activity breeds hope, passivity breeds despair." Ok, I thought, I agree that makes sense. She explained that it began with her own grandparenting experience and the realization that grandparenting requires a conscious effort and doesn't just happen. All those humorous quotes circulating the Internet and the fun and games promoted by lighthearted books with an emphasis on naturalness are terrific, but Lillian suggests through her research that it is more complicated than one thinks.

We continued talking as I accompanied her into the kitchen area where she got back to cooking while I perched myself on a nearby chrome stool. I scribbled some more notes as she multi-tasked, talking about grand-parenting as a job and the educational purpose of her book, all while dipping, rolling and browning the chicken breasts.

The evening was a delight, with great food and interesting conversation; besides me, other invited guests were a neighbor-friend, a son and two grandsons. Lillian, the gracious and thoughtful hostess, verbally acknowledged the friend with a celebratory nod on behalf of the recent sale of his house, then, both grandsons' upcoming birthdays and finally me with the passing of my bill. She even went to the trouble of having a printed copy of my bill at the table, designating the youngest child to read it aloud. How fitting to have a grandchild recite a paragraph about the preservation of the grandparent-grandchild relationship. I was truly touched by such a kind and most unexpected gesture.

Thoroughly enjoying each other's company, and wanting to extend our visit, we met the next morning for a walk. Lillian had told me about the freeway underpass to Butterfly Beach, just a few blocks from her house and I was anxious to see it for myself. We got sidetracked a few times visiting the gardens of the Music Academy of The West and the Biltmore Hotel, eventually arriving at the scenic, secluded Butterfly Beach. Circling back toward town we ended up on Coast Village Road and 'Peets' coffee where we settled at an outside corner table for two and the best latte I've ever had. We had so much to talk about and not enough time, as Lillian and I traded stories about our own grandchildren and some of the obstacles we have endured just to love them.

The visit was too short, yet I came away inspired and better informed on many levels than I had been before the experience. Lillian would sometimes quote an old show business saying, "always leave them wanting more." And that is exactly how I felt.

It wasn't until I met her and then read her book that I

realized the depth of Lillian's mission and her desire to offer a "blueprint" on the idea that grand-parenting is indeed serious business. Her motivation is to communicate that many people do not take grand-parenting seriously, often the role is devalued and it is not recognized as a conscious effort or job.

Yes, grandparents do have a choice about how active they wish to be in their grandchildren's lives. The family dynamics are different; there are also more people involved now, not just the two generations and the grandparents are not in charge. Grandparents must balance influencing a child's life and supporting the parents in their role. Lillian says of her own experience, "It is so exciting to give them ideas."

Lillian's background as a psychologist influences her analytical and thoughtful point of view on the subject. She states that to be a grandparent is "important work and most of the time it has to be intentional and planned."

In 1996, growing from her passion for the subject and demand, her book "The Essential Grandparent" was published. She suggests grandparents and their families are an endangered species and grandparents truly are more essential to a family than ever before. Lillian emphasizes that "I wrote this book to tell you why you are needed and of the great opportunity you have been given to influence the future."

Lillian explains some of the issues that have created changing dynamics of family life today. Divorce, daycare, distance all contribute to weakening the connection of the extended family, particularly the grandparents. "More families are socially isolated. All of this has resulted in a crisis for our grandchildren." Grandparents can intervene by giving time, affection and attention, ultimately making a difference. Lillian goes on to state, "Research supports the importance of this message by providing evidence that caring adults make a difference in children's lives."

As a psychotherapist, Lillian counsels many patients who are grandparents and have experienced and valued time with their own grandparents. The common thread between all of them, according to Lillian, is the "abiding love and longing far into adulthood, for the unconditional love and comfort they once received from them." Lillian states that she has interviewed hundreds of people and she happily reports that there is an enormous outpouring of love and gratitude because of the vital contribution from grandparents. A common theme often heard from grandchildren is: "I would have never made it without my grandparents." Grandparents' influence on a child is immeasurable; they provide complete acceptance and are instrumental in building a child's self-esteem. An example from Lillian's book from a young man who succeeded in spite of abusive parents, reinforces this point. "I didn't get admiration or encouragement from my parents, but my grandma said, 'you can do anything, Jimmy.' It was security, and unconditional love with no expectations. I didn't have to earn it."

As important as grandparents are to children, those children are equally important to grandparents. Lillian says that "nurturing the next generation is our rightful emotional task." She discusses the emotional quality of life because of involvement with youth and the reciprocal love and admiration that grandparents receive from grandchildren. "Self-esteem and self-confidence are closely linked to the feeling of being loved and being lovable."

In Dr. Carson's book, an ongoing theme is to communicate the "essential" message through the use of various examples that propose grandparents stay involved and not become complacent; she says it best in her own words:

> "Loving our grandchildren is usually not difficult, but we must do more than feel it. We've got to show it, too. Feeling love in our heart for a child is not enough. We need to express our love through words and actions, being ever mindful of what we say and do, because it matters."

Once grown, these grandchildren remember the demonstration of unconditional love through time spent together. Her last sentence describes how the content of the relationship builds "a loving, lasting friendship with grandchildren that enables them to soar as individuals."

In summary, Dr. Carson challenges the reader to engage in some soul searching about what it is that truly enriches one's life. For her it is being an active grand-parent within the cycle of life. "I fervently believe that active and involved grand-parenting holds a key to our health and that of our children and grandchildren." Besides passing on values, wisdom, history and tradition, Dr. Carson suggests that "we grandparents provide the nation's social glue." It is a silent code of responsible grand-parenting. We can all agree children are indeed our future as we are part of theirs with a mutual dependency. And as Dr. Carson reminds us, "you are essential."

My belief is that a child's, as well as an adult's emotional health is just as important as physical health; maintaining a consistent relationship with grandparents is crucial for both. The stability, security, and unconditional love provided by grandparents to a child fosters self-esteem, confidence and paves the way by laying the foundation to successful interpersonal relationships. Grandparents are the link to past and present, imparting wisdom, ancestry, traditions and an abundance of nurturing.

I don't know for sure if there is a shortage of caring adults for children in the world, but I do know there can never be such a thing as too many adults that care. Those children who are fortunate enough to have grandparents who participate in their lives should consider themselves blessed.

Professor Jack Westman from the University of Wisconsin wrote a most relevant article expressing his view of grandparenting, which with his permission, I wish to share.

GRANDPARENTHOOD

Jack C. Westman, M.D., Professor Emeritus, Department of Psychiatry, University of Wisconsin-Madison

A seven-year-old girl said about her grandmother: "She's old on the outside but she acts like she's young on the inside." She hit the nail on the head!

Most of us older adults remain active today with some of us still working into our seventies. Even those of us who retire during our sixties may spend as much as one-third of our lives after retirement with our families sometimes encompassing even five generations.

By the middle of the next century as the "baby boomers" are the elderly, the entire United States will resemble present-day Florida in the proportion of the population composed of older adults. In 1790 less than two percent of the population was over 65. In 1990 that figure was twelve percent; by 2030 it will be over twenty percent.

Living longer means that more of us now lead three lives: first as children, second as adults with careers and most likely as parents, and third as retirees from careers — and for most of us as grandparents. During each of these lives we continually discover and learn new things. We find sides of ourselves that we did not know existed. Our third life is a time for discovering new talents and creative possibilities in our inner worlds. It is a time for applying the wisdom of the ages to ourselves. It is a time for discovering the full meaning of life and for preparing for the future, whatever that may be.

Being a grandparent means different things. Although grandparenting is not the dominant aspect of most of our lives, it is an aspect that is more important than most of us realize. For some of us who are actively raising our grandchildren, it is the most important part of our lives. Unfortunately, an increasing number of us are doing just that today. Some of us are estranged from our children and from our grandchildren because of strife in our families. But most of us live at some distance from our grandchildren and manage to maintain an active role in their lives though the mail, the telephone, and visits.

As grandparents we have important symbolic and practical functions in our cultures. We are important simply for what we mean as the oldest living representatives of our families. We can be a matriarch or a patriarch for our families. Our roles as family historians, mentors, and role models can confer status and respect on us.

Without grandparents, there is no tangible family line. Children who have had no contact with grandparents miss knowledge of their ancestry. They may not be able to muster a confident sense of the future as concretely represented by the fact that older people have seen their futures become the present and the past.

As grandparents we are the links to the past in our families. We can recall when the parents of our grandchildren were young, not always to their liking! We are the repositories of information about our genealogies (we are well advised to record as much of that as we can). That information often becomes useful material for themes that our grandchildren write in school, and sometimes it flowers into full fledged writing about our family trees.

As grandparents we can provide advice to our children that is hopefully appreciated. That is best done tactfully and when asked for! We can bring our families together and foster and maintain communication between them. We can play healing roles in assuaging the challenges, hurts, and disappointments in our families. In doing so we need to carefully avoid stirring up difficulties, the potential for which especially lies just beneath the surface in in-law relationships. We are the conveyers of traditions in our families and in our cultures.

We have much to offer our families and our communities. We are the people who have been there. Whatever wisdom is should lie in us. We can see through the posturings of our everyday world. We can identify with the lifestream and the cycles of human existence. We know what really is important and what is not. We know that disappointments, heartaches, and pain are natural parts of life. We know that life goes on without us. We have been a part of history and often have an interest in learning more about the past. We have seen enough to know that everything is not sensible and rational. We have had enough dreams and life experiences to know that the mystical may be more real than the rational. We have learned that whatever it is — good or bad — it will pass.

If we have been reasonably wise in the conduct of our own lives, we have attended to our physical health and to our spiritual and emotional needs. We know that our bodies age, that our minds fail, but that our inner I remains the same throughout our lives. This is why we feel old in our bodies and minds but not in our spirits. This is why we really do not feel that the image in the mirror accurately reflects who we are. We truly know that we can be old on the outside but young on the inside. If we think about it, we can recognize that the present moment in truth is the "eternal now." In order to sharpen the vitality of our lives, we are well advised to manage our diets and to engage in regular physical exercise so that we can help our bodies serve us as well as is possible and so that we do not work against the efforts of our bodies to be healthy.

We also have the luxury of living our lives more or less as we wish. We have more control over our schedules because of the relinquishing of the responsibilities of the workplace. We have time to reflect and to enjoy the simple things in life. We can take time to appreciate the pleasures of simply being alive. We can enjoy the clouds, the trees, the flowers, and the smell of the air. We also can devote our time and energies to helping those who are less fortunate. Most importantly we can relive and resolve the past in our memories and reveries. The past is part of our lives today. We know what it feels like to lapse into the past as if it is the present. Our storehouse of memories leads most of us to relinquish the wish to live our lives over again.

We gain profound meaning in life from the love and respect of our juniors. The attachment between grandparent and grandchild is second in emotional power only to the bond between parent and child. The arrival of a grandchild usually triggers a dormant instinct to nurture in us. This is accompanied by joy in the birth or adoption of our grandchild; by recalling our own experiences as a parent and as a grandchild; and by thoughts about continuity of our own lives in the next generation.

Our grandchildren have as much to offer us as we have to offer them. We can enjoy pleasures with them without the responsibilities of rearing them. The love and attention we give them builds their self-esteem. Their interest in our company and in our stories reminds us of our importance to our families. We offer each other the sense of belonging not only to our families but to the human family.

As grandparents and as senior citizens, we are gaining an increasing amount of power in our society not only in the political arena but in the moral leadership of our society. We really do have much to offer even though there is a tendency to disparage the elderly. This is not the fact in the power structures of our society, however, to wit the number of people in their seventies and eighties in political office. We can advocate for the interests of the elderly, not only of our own but of those of us who are subjected to elder ageism and abuse. But most importantly we are aware of the interests and needs of future generations. We are in a position to be powerful advocates for children and parents. Because we are not motivated by advocacy for children that really is advocacy for adults, we can truly advocate the interests of children.

As grandparents, we are crucial resources for our families. But the art of grandparenting requires commitment, understanding, practice, and perseverance. We can offer approval, loving delight of our grandchildren, and reliable support for our own offspring. We are the link between the past and the present and even the future! It is through our grandchildren that we and humanity itself flow in the stream of life.

The philosopher Robert Nozick said it well:

We all might seriously weigh spending our penultimate years in endeavors to benefit others — in adventures to advance the cause of truth, goodness, beauty, or holiness — not going gentle into that good night or raging against the dying of the light but, near the end, shining our light most brightly.

Nobody can do for little children
what grandparents do.

Grandparents sort of sprinkle stardust
over the lives
of little children.

~alex haley

Four

EFFECTS ON GRANDPARENTS : WHEN ACCESS IS LOST

Grief, frustration, confusion, helplessness, and even anger are common emotions shared by ostracized grandparents. My desire to explore the effects on grandparents following lost visitation led me to an article written by Dr. Cartwright, an educational and counseling psychologist at McGill University. He has further studied the phenomenon of (PAS) and in his compelling article, "Expanding the Parameters of Parental Alienation Syndrome" for *The American Journal of Family Therapy*, described the emotion as akin to that of a "missing child" because there is no closure, you are just left dangling, wondering, waiting, hoping. The cliché "hanging from a cliff" fits. The child is out there, sometimes close by, sometimes far away, but even if we know where they are, we can't get to them, because we are not allowed access. But, maybe we will be someday, so we wait. That's where the frustration accumulates. The confusion is ongoing; we continually attempt to figure out how we got in the situation we're in, searching and hoping to discover the missing puzzle piece; we mostly have no idea why we can't be with our grandchildren. We feel helpless knowing that despite the parents' perception of a problem, the grandchildren still need us and we need them. But because of obstacles such as laws, finances, and unreasonable individuals, we are unable to change the situation. We feel angry and confused, but most of all, we ache to see our grandchildren.

Over and over in our heads we play the entire relationship we once had with these grandchildren, the happy memories of bonding with the ones we love so deeply. Remembering our time with them sustains us during our grieving; it is their voices, the memory of their smell, touch and laughter that lives in our hearts and is ours to hold, cherish and pine for.

The flip side is recalling how our future was stolen from us by circumstances out of our control. My experience with talking to grandparents is that they have gone to great lengths to make amends with the parents by taking responsibility for any discord they may have caused. They continue to make futile attempts to reconcile. They don't dispute that parents are the ones in charge; their intention is not to take over or supersede parental authority. They just want the opportunity to love the child. A point of discussion is the perplexing notion that the outcome is so disproportionate to the event. The punishment in these cases does not fit the crime; it is far too extreme. Dr. Kornhaber, one of the nation's foremost experts on grandparenting issues, said it best: "Get rid of the problem, not the person." This is a dilemma that is heavily discussed between disenfranchised grandparents as they continue their search for solutions and solace.

The emotions and stages of dealing with this separation are similar to coming to terms with a death, but without the finality; similar to suffering through divorce, yet divorce involves consenting adults. The emptiness persists; something is missing; a piece of our heart is gone. And because helpless little children, dependent on others, are involved, it is even more inconsolable and unending.

We feel condemned and unjustly treated. We have suddenly been eliminated from our grandchildren's lives with little recourse: convicted without so much as a fair trial. Most of the time we don't get to defend ourselves or even learn the reason for the abolishment. Our greatest sorrow is for the child. What distresses me most and is the origin of my deepest pain and heartbreak is my overwhelming concern for the feelings of the child. Don't they get a vote on whom they get to love? Don't their feelings count? What about consideration for their loss and abandonment? Are their little hearts so insignificant? As adults, we have usually developed strategies, successful or not, for coping with the unfairness of life, but children, probably not so much. The personal loss of the grandparents is compounded by concern for the child's welfare. Most grandparents agree that it is worry for the child that hurts the most.

A common stress in this group of grandparents is suffering in silence. They hold their discomfort and details of the family dysfunction inside, feeling humiliated. Grandparents believe it is a reflection on them when their grown children become alienated. Once they are able to confide in others who share their situation, who understand that blame can be disputed, then the healing can commence; the pressure eases, bringing some relief.

Feeling discontent and unfulfilled manifests itself in different ways. For example, I find myself feeling a twinge of anguish when I see grandparents with their grandchildren; it is a reminder that I no longer have that. Two of the most unattractive feelings are envy and jealousy, which are difficult to admit and can surface when we want something that another has. I am happy for my friends who are grandparents, yet I find it too painful to discuss and hear all the details. For instance, when I see a photo of someone's grandkids, I have to mentally distance myself as a form of protection; the imaginary shield begins to rise ever so gently. Facing the fear and hurt in my loss is a daunting task; somehow, I put on a brave face and carry on.

One habit I have not broken is looking at every dark haired boy in Jacob's age group, no matter where I am. I know it's not him, but I still find myself hoping it is. This seems to be instinctual, it's so automatic. What goes through my mind: If I could just hug him and hold him for a minute.

Once during a yoga class, a little boy of about nine laid his mat next to mine for his practice with his mother. He had brown hair and was about the same stature as Jacob. I felt the tears well up in my eyes and I visually searched for another place for my mat, but there was none. As long as I didn't acknowledge him, I could get through the class. I struggled with polar opposite emotions, either ignoring him or pretending that he was Jacob and that we were enjoying a shared activity together. I floated between the two, wishing it was him and wishing it was not and that he would disappear. Sometimes it's just easier not to feel the pain. The road to healing, as I have learned is to go ahead and experience the feelings, accept them and then utilize our resources and coping skills toward a more peaceful and contented state of being. The circumstance is ongoing, and I do what I can to live with it, such as writing in a journal especially for Jacob to have one day. Reaching out to others to offer assistance and in turn accepting support are powerful healing tools. I took Lillian Carson's advice, from her book, to heart and gave myself permission to restore myself, and seek balance. This is a daily challenge.

Shared Stories About Losing Access From Grandparents:

Grandmother M.

Grandmother M. in a recent email stated her assessment of the grandparent predicament. "How about going back to the very beginning-when access is threatened! I believe it begins then-the chronic underlying uncertainty that causes one to feel they are walking on eggshells. I often feel that I am caught in the middle of a 'damned if I do, damned if I don't' situation. This has happened to me: The parents get mad whenever I do for the child and also if I don't. So, the child feels the strain and loss and so does grandma as her cortisol goes sky high, thus effecting my health. I have had five years of this-never knowing IF I will be allowed to do anything with the grandchildren; and the grandchildren being told, 'see how grandmother prefers other grandchildren, that's why she won't take you places'. I become so frustrated and always feel off balance. I make plans and buy tickets only to find that at the last minute the kids are unavailable. I feel so hopeless because I believe it is hurtful to the children, always living in a state of inconsistency. I am not willing to play the blame game. So what does a grandparent do?"

Stress and the Spare Tire:

Speaking of cortisol, much has been discussed in the media about belly fat lately. Research explains that chronic stress causes our body to secrete excessive amounts of the hormone cortisol, and too much cortisol triggers cravings for high fat, high sugar foods. Cortisol stimulates fat production deep in the abdomen, the worst place to put on pounds. In a recent AARP magazine article about stress, Elissa Epel, Ph.D., from her study explains that stress influences where fat gets deposited on our body, so it's logical that stress reduction should minimize it; all the more reason to find productive ways to deal with the stress brought on by the disconnect we experience with our loved ones.

Stress And Contribution To Disease

Grandmother J.

Grandmother J. shared with me her feelings about the sudden estrangement from her son, his wife and three children. "This is the worst thing I have ever experienced. I feel like a shell; this really broke my heart. I worked so hard to be a good parent — then had a son that did this? I felt like a failure, what could I have done or not done?"

J. reflected on the past as she continued, "My son and I always had such a close relationship and our daughter-in–law as well. Then all of a sudden he started making excuses whenever I asked to see the kids. I kept playing over again in my head anything I could think of that might have ignited the situation. All I came up with was a confrontation from him during a recent vacation, when he refused to allow me to give the kids a souvenir that I had bought. He informed me that he was imposing this new rule: no gifts unless it was birthday or Christmas, and then threatened, 'the law is on my side on this.' The distance grew wider with all phone contact coming to a halt (his idea), and only occasional e-mails were exchanged. During the no-visit period, I signed up to volunteer at the children's school and when one of the kids happily mentioned it to the parents, they became furious and accused me of brokering time. My own son, treating his parents with so much disrespect, was mind-boggling. It was going on six months when I had to call him out of necessity to inform him that I had cancer."

J. believes that the stress she experienced may have contributed to her illness. She went on, "I will never know if it was because of my health crisis that he came to his senses but soon after my husband and I were once again seeing the kids. This time, our son has changed the dynamics of the relationship; we no longer are allowed to have sleepovers. Now the visits are structured and at a minimum; his warmth has turned to polite distance. All we can do is go along, and play the game."

J. reiterated her experience, "It is the worst thing in the world to take away grandkids and not say why; don't do this to a person; you don't heal; it can put your own health at risk when feeling resentful, it's not good."

Depression And Disconnection

Grandmother JLM

This grandmother is suffering the consequences of her grandchild moving out of state. Actually, her only grandson and his parents moved to the East Coast from the West Coast, suddenly and without purpose. JLM said of her four-year-old grandson: "We were so close, I saw him three times a week and now it's maybe two times a year. I never thought this would happen -- that they would move away on such a whim. I'm not getting over it; I think about him everyday." She said she sometimes feels like she has lost her way and purpose in life.

We agreed nobody understands the feeling unless they are a grandparent. She expressed her gratitude for the ongoing support of the Lost Access group. JLM even pondered the thought of moving closer to her grandson, but reminisced how hard it would be to leave our group. She said, "It is not so simple to move, so maybe there is still hope of persuading the family to move back. There is a lack of stability about the circumstances and a feeling of uneasiness that disturbs me." Grandmother JLM began to cry. "Holidays are not the same." I asked her about the ways these emotions manifested themselves, and she explained the overwhelming sadness that turns into crying and sleeplessness. Grandmother JLM feels fortunate to have the child remain in her life, however, it is difficult to carry on a phone conversation with a four year old, especially when that is your only means of communication.

ABOUT STRESS:

A common thread that connects the grandparents denied access to grandchildren is emotional stress. The circumstances causing these unwanted physical and emotional responses are overwhelming for them. Some of the physical reactions that grandparents have shared are: high blood pressure, heart racing, headache, fatigue, sleeplessness, stomach upset and so on. The emotional markers of their struggle are anxiety, sadness, lack of concentration, anger, sleep disruption, and depression.

Stress arises as a result of the following: frustration, conflict, change and pressure. Grandparents endure all of them. Frustration happens in any situation in which the pursuit of some goal is thwarted. A grandparent's goal to engage in visitation is suddenly eliminated and therefore thwarted. Change is an alteration that requires adjustment. Grandparents in our group experience a major change, like ending their role and time with a beloved grandchild, which is a hard pill to swallow. Conflict can occur when making a choice between two unattractive goals. The grandparent can either comply and stay away from the grandchild, or disagree, which may include confrontation; both reactions cause conflict and usually trigger anxiety, depression and physical symptoms. Pressure is the demands and expectation that a person must behave in a particular way, i.e. rules and roles to follow in order to maintain the relationship. Grandparents have stated more than once that they feel like they are "walking on eggshells."

In a study done by Segerstrom and Miller: "The Psychological Stress to the Human Immune System," also in the same section from the *AARP* magazine, they suggest that stressors that turn a person's world upside down and appear to offer no hope for the future probably have the greatest psychological and physiological impact. The most chronic stressors happen when a person feels no sense of control and/or the situation seems endless. These stressors resulted in the most global suppression of immunity. The longer the stress lasts the more negative changes occur.

The study also addressed age as a factor. Age does affect a person's vulnerability to stress-related diseases and led to decreased immune function. It seems that illness and age make it harder for the body to regulate itself.

This research applies to the state of being disenfranchised grandparents who have formed strong attachments to their grandchildren only to have them severed. Grandparents are usually older adults whose age factor is compounded by the endlessness and hopelessness of their situation.

Grandparents finding themselves in this situation are a prime target for stress disorders, therefore recognizing and taking steps to manage the stress is of vital importance to their health. Remember grandmother J. who became ill with cancer during her family crisis? She intuited that her disease may have been influenced by the stress of separation from her grandchildren. The grandparents that I counsel and who attend the support group I run have already taken the first step in relieving stress by making contact and reaching out for help. Building a support system is critical to emotional healing because it provides a venue in which to confide your feelings. The choice is entirely up to each individual as to how they manage their stress. Some choose to avoid whenever possible, and others make changes in their responses to the stressful events. Self-talk, our perceptions of the event and how we assess it, and what we think about it, all determine how we feel. I believe no one solution can relieve the stress but the combination of many coping strategies can help achieve a place of physical and emotional balance in one's life. None of this is easy and it requires ongoing effort to get through it. I have gathered some simple stress management information and included it in the following list.

Stress Management:

1. Accept the sadness when it strikes and allow some time to experience the pain. Avoid suffering in silence and letting it build up.

2. Don't take things personally. This is a tough one. The alienation is not about you, but about the other person's issues.

3. Reach out and assist others in need. Getting out of ourselves now and then helps us as well as others.

4. Writing in a journal has great healing power. Very cathartic, and yes tearful.

5. Socialize with one or many, whichever suits.

6. Do something you enjoy alone and just for you. Treat yourself to pampering, a movie, a book, music, indulge in a favorite food, explore new territory.

7. Exercise. I can't emphasize this enough for

overall health; it is the best tension buster and my favorite way to manage my ups and downs.

8. Meditate. Create time for calm and relaxation. Breathe deeply and slowly. Visualize something beautiful and calming.

9. Focus on what is good in your life. Be mindful.

10. Seek professional counseling or a support group.

11. Practice healthy eating and lifestyle.

Creating a Hopeful Situation

Grandparents can be proactive by continuing to send gifts and cards to not only their grandchildren but to the parents as well. Let the parents know that you acknowledge their existence and respect their role as the parent of your grandchildren. Don't give up; do everything possible to re-connect even it means humbling your ego. This is not a time to satisfy the need to be right. Gather all your resources and practice patience, empathy, forgiveness, faith, kindness, love and understanding. We are still grandparents, if only in our souls, and we remain connected within the universe no matter what anyone else does to prevent the physical presence.

We can derive a sense of accomplishment when we put our energy into something productive. Stay involved in something that you love, like work or a project. Find satisfaction in other areas of your life. Never forget, but don't be consumed by the tragedy. It is more about seeking balance because the stress can take over and keep us out of focus and alignment, preventing us from pursuing our life purpose. We end up losing ourselves and become powerless. We might want to be mindful that these grandchildren are only one piece of who we are and maybe it is unhealthy to allow our entire life to revolve around one person. And, yes, it is devastating to miss that one piece, but we must go on and in so doing, fill ourselves up in other ways. There are many components that make up who we are. Finding joy within ourselves in the midst of turmoil is a monumental task that seems to require super powers, and it often does.

If nothing
is
going
well,
call
your
Grandmother.

~ italian proverb

Five

Effects On Child : When Attachment Is Broken

By monitoring a grandparent support hotline, website and discussion group for my non-profit grandparent organization, I hear so many stories about family dynamics, especially attachment issues and different forms of alienation. The grandparents I come in contact with share that their primary concern is for the welfare of the children caught in the middle of adult conflict. They often report examples of brainwashing, with the parents hoping the grandparent[s] become alienated when the grandchildren adopt the parents' attitudes. Those I communicate with are distressed about their grandchild's emotional well-being when suddenly separated from a grandparent with whom they had grown attached.

PAS AND GAS:

PARENTAL ALIENATION SYNDROME AND GRANDPARENT ALIENATION SYNDROME

I have personally observed parental brainwashing, and the attempted alienation of my own grandchild. He reported that his mother had disparaged me [my words] by telling him that I was kind of crazy, not his real but instead "pretend" grandmother and that I was going to steal him and his half brother. He once said to his father, "I love her and miss her, but mom gets mad." His little brother once sadly admitted, "I miss her voice." This is just one example of alienating behavior and how it can foster fear and anxiety in the children who want to love their grandparents, but the price becomes too high and the negative consequences too great.

Grandparents communicated similar incidents that they had experienced. The excuses the parents gave to the children were creative to say the least. The grandparents sometimes learned through the grapevine what the children were told when the grandparents abruptly went missing. Sometimes the grandchildren had been told by the parents that grandma and grandpa moved far away, or grandma was sick or simply too busy. There were also parents who told their children that the grandparent had made poor choices or was not being nice to mommy and telling lies.

Brainwashing of children by one parent, especially during a divorce and custody battle, has been popularized by the label created by Dr. Richard Gardner, which is PAS or "Parental Alienation Syndrome." There is a difference between PAS and Parental Alienation. Parental alienation is when a parent attempts to sabotage the relationship between the child and the other parent, relatives included, through various tactics. PAS or parental alienation syndrome takes it a step farther and the child joins the alienating parent against the target person, which poses a greater threat to the destruction of the parent-child relationship. Sometimes the damage is reversible and sometimes it is permanent.

I wondered about this type of vilification and how it applies to extended family members such as grandparents. The parental alienation behavior has always been in existence; however, it is now growing and is recognized as a legitimate condition, named and labeled PAS.

Does it seem plausible this syndrome might be applied to include grandparents? Could there be a GAS, Grandparent Alienation Syndrome? I suppose any number of circumstances could be applicable. I discovered from my investigation that parents can and do program children in such a way that they become alienated from the target person and sometimes it evolves into PAS, which combines the child's contribution to the denigration. This is a more serious form of brainwashing. I know grandparent alienation exists, so it seems the syndrome with the child's participation is possible with grandparents as well as parents.

My research brought me first to an article called "Expanding the Parameters of Parental Alienation Syndrome" by Glenn F. Cartwright, of McGill University.

Professor Cartwright discusses the short, medium and long term effects to the victims of PAS. Besides the non-custodial parent, the grandparents also experience anguish over the loss of the child through sudden dismissal. The child experiences great loss, similar to a death of a parent, grandparent and any other significant relatives, all at once. Professor Cartwright believes the loss is more "staggering" than an actual death of a parent because the child is unable to "acknowledge" or "mourn" the loss and it therefore becomes a "major tragedy of monumental proportions" in his[her]life. He calls these short term consequences.

"The medium term effects concern the continued absence [as opposed to initial loss] of the lost parent [and grandparents] and the effects it has on the child's development. Ordinary children who have grown up without a parent or grandparent often report 'something missing' in their childhood. What is lost, of course, is the day-to-day interaction, learning, support, and love that normally flows from parents and grandparents. While in the case of death such a loss is unavoidable, in the case of PAS such a loss is entirely avoidable and therefore inexcusable."

For the long term effects, Professor Cartwright suggests "that everyone involved in PAS suffers some degree of distress over the long term." He compares the feelings parents and grandparents experience as being similar to what is experienced when a child goes missing. "Grandparents suffer needlessly and often seriously." Dr. Richard Gardner, who first defined PAS, wrote of the cases of at least two grandmothers, "in otherwise good health, who died of broken hearts, figuratively, over the loss of their grandchildren."

Professor Cartwright emphasizes that it is the child who suffers most. He explains that during the first stage the child experiences the loss of a parent and or grandparent and is subjected to continual denigration of them by the alienating parent. All of the fond memories of them are "deliberately and systematically destroyed."

During the second stage, after some time has passed, the child begins to have feelings of guilt, realizing they wrongly rejected the lost family member. Often a backlash develops against the alienating parent.

Professor Cartwright quotes from an article written by a colleague, Goldwater, about long term effects of alienation.

"When such a child becomes an adult, the awareness of the enforced absence of the alienated parent for those many years may have a devastating impact and leave long-term feelings of guilt and loss. The alienating parent may then suffer the wrath his child feels for having precipitated this loss, and be in turn shut out of the child's life."

There are many factors that contribute to the seriousness of the emotional problems that may develop. Professor Cartwright summarizes that in order for children to make a successful adjustment from emotional problems they face an enormous task, for instance, avoiding repercussion of the alienating parent, forgiving and re-establishing the relationship with the lost parent or grandparent [if they are willing and alive] and working to restore lost memories. There is a great deal of emotional strain put upon the child as they go about making up for lost time.

Further research is needed to follow PAS children and to determine long term effects as they enter adulthood.

Cartwright concludes: "The problem of parental alienation syndrome is much more serious than previously imagined. Viewed in this light, the problem of PAS appears to be extremely serious. We often speak of the preserving family values, but even disintegrated nuclear families have values and rights (like child visitation) which must be preserved and respected to prevent further disintegration and total collapse. To do less is to sacrifice entire generations of children on the alter of alienation, condemning them to familial maladjustment and inflicting on them lifelong parental loss."

Grandparents may want to stand on high alert during turbulent times, because they could be on shaky ground. They often find themselves in a risky position, wanting to support their own child and concurrently remain amicable to the ex, so finding a neutral position is almost impossible. The child begins to lose all things familiar and grandparents on either side of the family could be the next target and eventually may no longer be there to provide the glue for the family.

Divorce And Grandparent Poison

Dr. Richard Warshak in his book "Divorce Poison" further addresses the alienation and hate that occurs by association. Dr. Warshak states that "divorce poison delivers a cruel blow to the extended family." He refers to Dr. Gardner's statement about the "spread of animosity," which is when "children regard as enemies not only the hated parent but everyone associated with that parent, including grandparents. As a result children lose contact with one-half of their family and their heritage."

Dr. Warshak explains when there is divorce poison, the children experience tremendous conflict about showing their love toward grandparents. Dr. Warshak said, "In a surprising number of families, divorce results in the total rupture of relations between an ex-spouse and the former in-laws. At first the children shun the extended family in order to show loyalty to the favored parent." Eventually the children become so brainwashed that they come to believe that the rejected grandparents are deserving of contempt. In these cases the parents are so wrapped up in their own problems they ignore the child's feelings and their best interests. The alienating parent many times will break off all ties and relations to the former in-laws and the child goes along with it.

"Alienated children succumb to a type of tribal warfare. They categorize every relative as either ally or enemy. No one can be neutral," says Dr. Warshak. Neutrality is therefore, perceived as disloyalty.

According to Dr. Warshak, children are exposed to various conditions that perpetrate brainwashing. Isolation is a form of the disconnecting process, such as separating the child from the grandparent. Dr. Warshak says, "First isolation breeds dependence. Second, it prevents exposure to competing views of reality. Isolation removes the child from the influence of people who would counteract the effects of bad-mouthing and bashing."

Fear is another condition developed by an alienating parent because it increases psychological dependence on the parent that is doing the bashing. A child will turn on a grandparent in order to self-protect against the wrath of an angry parent. Dr. Warshak explains that, "when a child observes his mother vent her anger in an irrational, uncontrolled manner his main concern is to avoid becoming her next target." In an example from the book, an angry mother finishing a tirade directed at her former mother-in-law while the child was present, turned to her son and said, "'Grandma is a mean old witch. Right?' *How was he to respond?* He correctly perceived that his mother was out of control. He had just witnessed a verbal assault on a grown-up who refused to see things her way. Although he adored his grandma, he certainly was not going to contradict his mother while she was in this state. His safest option was to join in his mother's hatred."

Dr. Warshak exposes some of the "common ploys" used to coerce children into rejecting grandparents. He calls it pejorative labeling, or manipulation of names which disrupts the identification and changes it. Children are like sponges, absorbing what they hear which becomes part of their belief system. According to Dr. Warshak, "Use a racial slur enough times and children will soon follow the example. The offensive word becomes part of their vocabulary. And without thinking, they absorb the hatred tied to the label. This is how we convert innocent children into racists. It is also how we turn them against formerly loved parents and their families."

When a parent is vindictive, he or she begins the process by making sure the child overhears when referring to the grandparent in a derogatory way, such as using the term "witch." The parents manipulate the children by showing approval whenever they follow the example by using the same term to refer to the grandparent. The child feels acceptance from the parents and eventually disrespect toward the grandparent. Dr. Warshak says, "Contemptuousness replaces love. After associating Granny with the label 'witch', their minds are tricked into thinking that somewhere along the line they decided for themselves that their grandmother was bad. The children lose sight of the origin of derogation." The assessment of Granny is not realistic but instead based on the mother's expression of "irrational anger."

Repetition is another form of brainwashing, the more we hear a word or idea the more familiar and comfortable it becomes. Dr. Warshak writes that "parental brainwashing can be thought of as propaganda in the home. Repetition also helps embed messages in the memory." The behavior is drilling something into the child's head over and over until it becomes rote memory, such as math. Says Warshak, "If a false impression-an unjustified denigration of a grandparent-is repeated enough times, it too can become second nature." The reality of the beliefs becomes distorted and blurred. Dr. Warshak refers to the

Cornell University research finding about how easy it is to implant false memories in young children.

Another tactic is to downplay the positive and accentuate the negative. Dr. Warshak writes that "a woman who was trying to alienate her children from their paternal grandparents had to downplay their significant contributions." He mentions that there are subtle ways of doing this such as "selective attention," where the parent focuses on what the grandparents haven't done and ignores all the good things that they do.

Encroachment is another tactic. The alienating parent attempts to reduce time spent with the grandparent by intruding on visits which keeps the child focused on that parent. Dr. Warshak gives an example of a dialogue that alienating parents will employ: "What's wrong?" or "Are you okay?" They want to plant in the child's head that it is expected for them to have problems when they are with the enemy. Another form of encroachment is sabotaging time with grandparents by rearranging activities that encroach on their scheduled time. Sometimes the parent will completely obstruct the activity such as taking them to a planned movie first before the grandparents, or buying them something bigger and better. Dr. Warshak says, "The children come to associate contact with the target [grandparent in this case] with disappointments such as prematurely ending a game, leaving in the middle of a movie, or missing a chance to go ice skating."

Dr. Warshak contends that once these irrationally alienated children become adults they continue to develop unresolved feelings or unresolved relationships. There is much that they have not processed because the feelings have not been acknowledged and therefore there is no healing or resolution. Their future personal relationships suffer since they are not aware of or enlightened about their own loving feelings, therefore they have less to give their spouses and families. When love is taken away from a child by depriving him or her of a loving grandparent, it spills into adult life and these children may treat their own children the same way. If a child is able to work through the issues and come to terms with the lost years, the adult child is apt to resent the brainwashing parent.

Perspective From A Family Law Attorney, Sheryl Edgar, Esq:

Parents have a right to parent their children as they see fit according to the Constitution of the United States. Neither the Federal Government nor the State Government can intervene absent a "compelling state interest." This means that the State cannot walk into your home and tell you what to do with your children unless the State feels compelled to protect the children. The Troxel decision (federal court) said that if a statute is drafted well, like the California Grandparent Statute and not vague, it would be considered "constitutional" for the State to come into the parents' home and say that they MUST let a grandparent visit. This is a roundabout way of saying that in some circumstances it would be detrimental to the children to sever a grandparent/grandchild relationship where a bond exists.

The State can always intervene where children are being abused, physically or emotionally. It would make sense that terminating a bonded grandparent/grandchild relationship could be considered emotional abuse by parents especially if motivated by anger or for arbitrary reasons. And if all the criteria of the statute are met, it would certainly not be in the child's best interest to terminate the relationship.

This gives credence to the needs of the child without specifically giving the child their own set of rights. The rights of children have been the subject of debate for an extended period of time. Parental autonomy must be respected unless that autonomy is detrimental to the child. Therein lies the legal battle we fight.

It would be interesting to have good solid data on the psychological impact of severing a grandparent/grandchild relationship as well as a study on whether or not children with doting grandparents have better self-esteem. I know I do because of my grandparents.

Sheryl L. Edgar, Esq.
Center for Children & Family Law
Orange, Ca.

Best Interests Of The Child

Santa Clara University:
Dr. Eleanor Willemsen Interview

April 2, 2007 I flew to Santa Clara, California which is near San Jose and just a short hour and fifteen minutes from John Wayne Airport in Orange County. I had read an article, "The Best Interests of the Child," written by the distinguished Professor Eleanor Willemsen and her husband Attorney Michael Willemsen for the Markkula Center for Applied Ethics within Santa Clara University, and wanted to meet her in person to discuss her work.

The piece caught my eye because of the title, "The Best Interests of the Child," and the references to the grandparent relationship, which I thought was relevant to my project. Because of my interest in the subject, Dr. Willemsen so kindly agreed to allow me to publish the article within this chapter. My original contact began through her university e-mail address, then we spoke by telephone and she graciously agreed to a personal interview. Santa Clara University, a Jesuit university, is located in the heart of Northern California and the Silicon Valley, just 40 miles south of San Francisco. It is known for its mission (on campus) Santa Clara de Asis. The grounds are beautifully landscaped, with lots of green grass, seasonal flowers and mature shade trees spilling onto the tiled roofs and porticos of the Spanish-style buildings. SCU has been called one of the most beautiful colleges in California. A department within the university is the Markkula Center for Applied Ethics, which is a nationally recognized resource for people and organizations wanting to study and apply an ethical approach to the crucial issues facing our world.

Dr. Willemsen, along with her husband, presented an in-depth analysis of the true meaning of the "best interests" standard of measurement on behalf of children's welfare.

Dr. Willemsen is a developmental psychologist and a qualified expert in the field of emotional development of children. Her study addresses attachment disorder in circumstances when children had developed a strong bond with significant adults in their lives, grandparents included. She was quick to point out that the research study had not specifically isolated the grandparent connection, and suggested a study of that nature could be a future possibility.

I asked Dr. Willemsen to further explain about "harm when a child loses ongoing intimate relationships." She emphasized that there is evidence over time that a child's social skills diminish, they become insecure, and there are cognitive effects. Also, when attachment is disrupted, professionals in the field don't spend time exploring outside elements, and other people, but rather are concerned with the security of the attachment.

We discussed possible solutions, and the notion of "Liberty Interests," came up, which is to bring the child standing [in a court of law] to be heard. Dr. Willemsen feels the least adversarial way for a court to examine a child's best interests in, for example, custody and visitation cases, is to give the child the right to representation. She would like to see more child advocates, such as a guardian ad litem or court appointed advocates, who are mandated by the states to represent children's liberty interests, giving them standing and some rights.

My trip was short yet productive and I came away with valuable information. I enjoyed my time with the professor, in the educational setting, exchanging personal stories, talking about ideas and quietly slipping in and out of the role of student. I frantically wrote notes as she casually and articulately dictated information as we sat in her tiny cluttered office. I was grateful for the condensed lecture about psychology and the law with relation to child attachment disorder. As I was leaving, I shared a personal observation that occurred whenever I visited my grandson at his home; he would cling to me and seemed oblivious to others around us. He was not interested in playing with the neighborhood child or interacting with his cousin and other grandma, instead he chose to remain close to my side and play with me. Dr. Willemsen enlightened me on her theory, which was, perhaps the child intuitively did not feel the relationship was stable and therefore, didn't want to leave. There was a fear of losing me that must have been present. It made sense, and all this time I just thought he liked me best. During the time we spent together we also came to recognize we shared the bond of being a grandparent.

"The Best Interest of the Child" is reprinted with permission by Dr. Eleanor Willemsen and Michael Willemsen, Esq.

When the Coast Guard plucked 6-year-old Elian Gonzalez from the sea last November, he became the subject of one of the more intense child custody dramas of recent times. His Cuban mother perished in the attempt to reach freedom in the United States, and at this writing, Elian is still being fought over by his Cuban father and his Miami relatives.

His grandmothers came from Cuba. The U.S. relatives met with the attorney general. A Florida family court judge asserted jurisdiction while the U.S. Immigration Service argued that this matter was purely one of immigration policy and law. The Supreme Court refused to resolve these squabbles.

Elian's case appears to be an extraordinary child custody conflict. Arguments about what is in his best interests intersect with immigration policy, federal and state procedural rules, and political agendas. But, as unusual as this case may seem, the ethical issues it raises are identical with those that arise routinely whenever the state is asked to take part in determining where a young child will live, who will care for him, and who else will have a continuing relationship with him supported by court-ordered visits.

Even if we agree that "best interests of the child" is the gold standard for deciding these questions, there is disagreement about how that test is to be applied. How does this "best interests" test interact with the rights of individual adults to establish and/or maintain nurturing relationships with the child and to make decisions that promote their own goals for a happy and productive life? To assist us in thinking about these issues, let us take a look at several examples.

Case 1: In 1968, a father fled Czechoslovakia with his two children and brought them to the United States. Several years later he died of cancer. The neighbors who had cared for the children during the father's illness disputed custody with the Czech mother [In re B.G. (1974) 11 Cal.3d 679]. The California Supreme Court said that the trial court could award custody to the neighbors only if it found that an award of custody to the mother would be "detrimental" to the children; on rehearing, the trial court found detriment and gave custody to the neighbors.

Case 2: A birth mother withdrew her consent to the adoption of her daughter Haley on the last day of the six-month period when that action was possible and sought to regain custody from the prospective adoptive parents (In re Haley A. [1996) 49 Cal. App.4th 1351]. The California Court of Appeal found the withdrawal of consent timely and ordered Haley returned to the birth mother without considering the best interests of the child. The California Supreme Court granted review, but when Haley was three years old, the case was settled by an agreement for an open adoption whereby Haley remains with her adoptive parents and has visitation with her biological mother. Thus, the California Supreme Court never decided the issues before it in this case.

Case 3: In the famous Baby Jessica case, the birth parents sought custody from the prospective adoptive parents, claiming that the birth father had never been notified of his right to object to the adoption because the birth mother had named the wrong man as the father [In re B.G. C. (Iowa 1992) 496 N.W.2d 239]. Although the birth parents tried to reclaim Jessica within a few weeks of her birth, the case dragged on for two years, with the child in the custody of the prospective adoptive parents. Eventually, the court denied the adoption and gave custody to the birth parents, without regard to the best interests of the child.

Case 4: When a child of Native American ancestry was placed with a white couple, her tribe contested the adoption on the grounds that relatives who could teach her the tribal heritage should raise her [In re Bridget R. (1996) 41 Cal. App.4th 1483]. The California Court of Appeal rejected the claim, holding that the child had a constitutional right to maintenance of her established relationship with the adoptive parents.

Case 5: After a child's birth father committed suicide, the mother remarried, and she and the step-father tried to bar visitation by the deceased father's parents [In re Custody of Smith (Wash. 1998) 969 P.2d 21, cert. granted sub. nom. *Troxel v. Granville* (1999)]. Washington, where the family lived, has a statute permitting any person to petition for visitation on the basis of the best interests of the child, but the Washington Supreme Court held the statute unconstitutional and allowed the mother to bar visitation by the grandparents. The case is currently pending in the United States Supreme Court.

Case 6: Two lesbian women living in a committed relationship agreed that one would become pregnant, and they would raise the baby together as joint mothers. But when they split up years later, the biological mother refused to let the other woman visit the child [*Crandall v. Wagner* (1999) 71 Cal. App.4th 724]. The court held that visitation can be granted only in connection with a divorce, paternity, or juvenile dependency action. Since no such proceeding was pending, it could not award visitation regardless of the best interests of the child. As other California courts have done, it reserved resolution of this problem for the legislature.

Case 7: Following a divorce, a mother wanted to take a new job in a distant location, which would make it difficult for the father to continue regular and extensive visitation [Marriage of Burgess (1996) 13 Cal.4th 25]. The California Supreme Court said that the custodial parent has a right to move, and the visitation arrangements have to be adapted to the move. While the court can change custody because of the pending move, a custodial parent cannot be barred from moving on the grounds that the move will make visitation more difficult and thus is not in the child's best interests.

The Ethical Issues

The resolutions of these cases, though justified in some instances by the particular statutes or procedural issues before the court, are in fundamental conflict on when the courts should consider the best interests of the child and how to do so. The conflict is not at heart a legal one but an ethical one. Two categories of problems stand out.

The first is balancing the "best interests" test with claims of parental rights. Parents have a right to separate, divorce, and move. They have a right to direct the upbringing of their children, including the right to exclude others from that function. They also have procedural rights to contest custody, visitation, and adoption. But the assertion of any of these rights may conflict with the child's best interests.

The second category is whether determination of the best interests of the child means attending to everything that affects the child or whether certain considerations should be disregarded. Should the courts take into account that one party seeking custody has substantially more income and can give the child better schooling, better medical care, and a less dangerous environment? Should they look at other considerations—homosexuality, religion, race, ancestry, etc? What about "living in a free country" or being a member of an ethnic community to which one has ancestral ties? Or does "best interests" mean the interests of the child in nurture and care apart from these considerations?

Lessons from Developmental Psychology

Research in developmental psychology tells us that children need stability and security and are harmed when they lose their ongoing intimate relationships with those few adults who provide their nurture and care. A large literature in psychology documents the importance of these relationships of attachment between caregiver and child, especially for young children.

When these relationships are stable, they serve as a secure base from which the young child ventures forth into the world of other people, things, and events. Children who enjoy relationships of intimacy and security with their closest caregiver(s) in the first three years are more likely than those who do not to be curious and explore their environments. They are more likely to be friendly and successful relating to other children and new adult caregivers, better able to communicate, more able to play and learn independently, and more likely to grow up to have successful relationships in marriage and at work.

Psychologists and psychiatrists have taken this framework into the clinical realm. A good body of case material and descriptive studies of groups of people who have experienced loss of important ties demonstrate the existence of a pattern of problems now known as "attachment disorder." When there is disruption of an ongoing important relationship of attachment, the child responds with an increased need to control whatever relationships she has the opportunity to come by.

This she does in one of two ways: She may become preoccupied with getting and keeping the attention of caregivers, teachers, and friends at the expense of trying her own wings and building her self-confidence. Alternatively, she may dismiss the importance of relationships and concentrate on independent activities and achievements at the expense of having satisfying relationships.

Either of these patterns is associated with difficulties in adulthood with close relationships, parenting, and finding the healthy balance between independence and closeness that is the cornerstone of mental health. It is important to note that the child who appears to be handling a custody change with no problem may in fact be exhibiting the "dismissing" variation of attachment disorder.

Of course, children have needs other than close

attachment. It goes without saying that the placement and support package we create must provide for the child's food, shelter, clothing, health care, and education. The child must be safe in her home, and she must have the opportunity to develop her skills, interests, and character strengths. The emphasis here is on attachment because this is the domain of early development most commonly misunderstood, under-valued, and ignored by the legal system.

From the viewpoint of a developmental psychologist, early successful attachment becomes the working model of how to relate to other people while being an independent person, as well. We must protect children's rights to continue their close relationships with nurturing adults.

An Ethical Framework

How can we as a society proceed in situations of disputed child custody so that the child's best interests are paramount? And at the same time, how can we devise a system that restricts the custodial parent's right to reasonable autonomy only when this is essential to the child's opportunity for healthy development and stability in her most central nurturing relationships? We offer five general ethical principles:

Principle 1: We must respect the child as a person and acknowledge that she is the most vulnerable party in the proceeding. Thus, regardless of the circumstances that lead the child's custody to be at issue, her best interests must be the central concern of the state. It is a moral wrong to decide issues of child placement based on adult conflicts and injustices that may have stemmed from adult behavior without examining how these decisions may impact the child. The most important aspect of being a whole person when you are a small child is your opportunity to develop well.

Thus we are especially concerned when courts decide custody and visitation issues by principles that do not allow them to take the interests of the child into account. In the Baby Jessica case (In re B.G. C.), the court considered only that the birth father had been fraudulently deprived of his opportunity to assert a parental objection to adoption. It held that it could take no account of the child bonding and care with the prospective adoptive parents. In *Crandall v. Wagner* the court interpreted the California Family Code as providing no forum in which it could consider the child's best interests since the parties, being lesbian, had not married.

The decisions of the California Court of Appeal in Haley A. and the Washington Supreme Court in Custody of Smith also found reasons not to consider the best interests of the child. All assume that the child's rights, if any, are only those conferred by statute. We disagree, believing that a child has a natural right, and should have a constitutional right, to be nurtured at least on a par with the parent's right to parent.

Principle 2: The placement decision and visitation plans ultimately reached must take central account of the child's important relationships of attachment. There may be several of these, and arriving at a plan to preserve them all may be difficult. Nonetheless, these relationships matter, and they have great impact on development.

It would be unfortunate if, in the case involving grandparent visitation currently being considered, the United States Supreme Court strikes down the Washington law allowing such visitation where a relationship clearly exists, because a child's relationships need protection. The relationship may be with grandparents, as in the Washington case, but it can also be with a stepparent, with a long-term partner who never married the biological parent (or who can't marry her, as in Crandall), with an aunt or uncle, etc.

Principle 3: We must move swiftly to provide a placement plan that will offer the child a stable, long-term living situation. Young children develop rapidly. In infancy, the events of a few weeks can result in sea changes. In the toddler years, six months is a developmental stage. In the preschool period, a year is an eternity.

We must balance the due process rights of parents and other players in the case with the child's right to a have a dependable, secure placement that preserves her developmental progress to date and facilitates its continuation. It is of paramount importance that we modify our legal procedures to achieve this important goal.

Principle 4: Whoever is caring for the child in the role of a parent must be fit to parent. He, she, or they must be able to provide safety, food, shelter, medical care, and education for the child. This is a well-respected principle that has long been part of societal practice in child custody cases. Since our emphasis has been on the more psychological aspects of custody, we wish to acknowledge and endorse this fundamental rule.

However, we hasten to add a corollary to this principle: The relative fitness of competing candidates for custody ought to be evaluated on the basis of their fundamental abilities to organize and support a structure for providing the things a child needs. Factors that are often considered inappropriately include the relative wealth and status of the parties and the political or religious climates in which the parties live.

In our view race and ethnicity are equally irrelevant although we recognize that this is a point of controversy. There may be extreme cases in which any of these factors could impact parental fitness, such as snake handling as a religious practice, but these must be treated as exceptional situations. Otherwise fitness should be strictly viewed from the perspective of what the child needs to develop in a healthy way.

Principle 5: Our respect for family autonomy—the right of custodial parents to make decisions about the day-to-day conduct of their children's lives—must be constrained to prevent the severing of the child's important attachments. At times, extraordinary effort may be required from two or more parties in order that one of them can raise the child effectively with the continuing involvement with the other(s). This is not to say that the state should micro-manage child rearing on a day-to-day basis. What the state can do is protect children from serious psychological harm resulting from severed relationships that are centrally important to their lives.

In Elian's case, the principle of preserving established bonds would require his return to his father. Certainly in ordinary circumstances when a mother dies and the father is a fit parent, no one questions the father's right to custody. One newspaper columnist pointed out that if Elian's mother had been a Mexican fleeing poverty instead of a Cuban fleeing tyranny, Elian would have been returned in 24 hours, probably without publicity or any hearing. We acknowledge that Elian can be given a politically freer and more prosperous life in America. But we question to what extent these are legitimate considerations and doubt that, in any event, they outweigh established parent-child attachments.

Eleanor Willemsen, professor of psychology at Santa Clara University, and Michael Willemsen, an attorney specializing in appellate law, often work together on cases involving child custody disputes.

Strategies For Reconnecting

If you are not seeing your grandchild, then counteracting the brainwashing activities by taking direct action probably won't happen until everything blows over. In the meantime there are ways that you can continue to express your love to your grandchild assuming they are allowed to receive your mail. Continue to send cards and letters, acknowledge birthdays and holidays by sending gifts. Tape recordings and photos help keep the memories alive. If, however, contact is discouraged, I recommend sending cards and letters to the parent[s] as a means to re-connect with them. Right now they hold the keys to the kingdom, so if there is any way to make amends and re-establish a relationship, then do it. What have you got to lose? The child's welfare is at stake, and as a significant member of their family grandparents cannot afford to be passive.

Dr. Willemsen suggested a court appointed advocate as a means to preserve and protect children's rights when applying the best interest standard. This is a viable solution and worth grandparents getting involved in and actively pursuing.

Finally, grandparents may seek professional mediation and or legal counsel whenever they have standing as another solution to protect the negative consequences brought upon a child when they lose a grandparent with whom they have formed an attachment.

The child is deprived in almost every way when they are deprived of a relationship in which they have had an established bond such as with a loving grandparent.

The history of our grandparents is remembered not with rose petals but in the laughter and tears of their children's children.

It is into us that the lives of grandparents have gone.

~ charles and
ann morse

Six

Legislation: How I Passed My Bill

I consider myself an average citizen, only occasionally interested in politics, and not particularly savvy when it comes to civics and government. But my passion to change a current law that kept children, in certain circumstances, from seeing their grandparents propelled me into unfamiliar territory. The sudden loss of visitation with my grandson, with perhaps no future contact, acquainted me with the reality that the grandparent/child bond is at the mercy and whim of parents. This was my driving force in passing a bill in California that would at least let grandparents petition the courts for visitation rights.

Feeling the impact of my own situation, and seeking resolution, I consulted different attorneys who all agreed that I had no standing in a courtroom, no right to be heard, and consequently no case. Out of the group consulted, one attorney stood out because of her ability to think outside the box. Sheryl Edgar was compassionate and very much a child advocate; she gave me hope by tossing out the daring idea that my only recourse to see my grandson was to contact legislators and convince them to change the law. The very idea seemed foreign and crazy to me; I had no frame of reference, experience, expertise or background; I wasn't even sure who my representatives were.

I spent the next year learning as much as possible, mostly through trial and error. Sometimes I felt like I was spinning my wheels, and confronted more than my share of roadblocks. I walked the beaches, parks, community centers, circulating a homemade petition and successfully accumulated signatures, which was intimidating at first, but I received positive reinforcement each time someone signed and spoke a kind word. On one occasion, I had a helper, who acted as a Spanish translator which got us lots of kudos and signatures; another time, I found myself in the center of a Vietnamese village reunion, where I was warmly received. I sat on the grass under a large shade tree with all of the families, as they passed my clipboard from person to person, pausing here and there for occasional translation. One family, in another group, tried to give me money, others tried to feed me. Eventually, I totaled about 500 names, and impressive as that seemed, the legislators that I approached declined to add a grandparent bill to their package. I continued to write, call and visit more legislators outside my district; I traveled to the state capitol in Sacramento to knock on even more doors.

It didn't happen that year. Looking back, I am grateful for the experience, that ended up being my education, giving me the opportunity to have a practice shot. The rejection was tough, considering my already fragile state. I felt frustration, grief and sadness, desperately wanting to confide in someone who would understand because she or he had had a similar experience. As I stated in chapter two, there were no support groups in Orange County specifically for grandparents with visitation issues; which is why I started my own.

Each of us had different circumstances, but the theme of being alienated from our grandchildren was identical. We listened, shared and supported one another. It was great; we were on our way. As a product of the group, the organization was born. The e-mails coming in as a result of the website began to grow; these heartbreaking stories confirmed the overwhelming need for awareness and solutions to an expanding problem that was affecting the stability of the extended family. Hearing these personal accounts firsthand further ignited the fire inside me, motivating me to once again stir things up in Sacramento.

Next thing I knew, I was bombarding legislators with letters, phone calls and e-mails with suggestions of proposed legislation on behalf of the children/ grandparent connection. All I needed was one legislator to commit. As it turns out, the newly elected Assemblyman Van Tran of Costa Mesa enthusiastically committed to author and introduce a bill that would provide rights to grandparents, allowing them the ability to petition the court in the circumstance of stepparent adoption. This would open one more door that had been closed to all of the children who had once had an established bond and pre-existing relationship with a grandparent[s].

In January 2006 Assemblyman Tran met with me in his district office in Costa Mesa to discuss content of the bill. During our meeting, I asked his opinion about the rise in visitation issues and parental restrictiveness; he responded that it was the language of the current laws that contributed to the grandparent/grandchild disconnection. The statutes addressing grandparent rights allow this to occur. If laws were enacted to include regard for the child's true best interests, there would be less disruption in the extended family unit. We talked about balancing parental autonomy with "grandparents' rights," which in reality is the right of a child to continue to have a beloved grandparent in their lives. As the sponsor of the bill, I promised to devote all of my attention to seeing that it passed, assuring him that I was willing to work hard and actively participate in the process. This soon became my priority as I worked my schedule around AB 2517. As I stated earlier, my original motivation to change the law was personally driven. That all changed just as I was about to get involved with legislation because the adoptive father contacted me and brought me back into Jacob's life in the midst of his turbulent divorce proceeding with Jacob's mother. I now had my grandson back, yet I still wanted to go forward and pursue the task of legislating because I recognized a need and hoped others would benefit.

Sacramento is where California law is enacted, and the legislative administrative staff are key to getting things done. I grew to know Jennifer Tannehill, Assemblyman Tran's legislative director, through e-mails and frequent phone conversations. She deferred to me often as a source of information and education during the early planning stages for the bill's content and language to be drafted by the Legislative Council. In order to bring her up to speed, I provided her with research, articles, cases, resources in the field, models of other states, and personal stories. Soon she shared my passion and understanding for the situation that affected so many children's and grandparents' lives.

There is an established calendar that regulates both houses, the Assembly and Senate, to carry out legislative activity according to schedule. Once we narrowed down the most concise statement to convey the intent of the bill, the attorneys in the Legislative Counsel Office could begin drafting it with appropriate legal terminology.

Within a month, the official draft was a finished product and was formally introduced during "First Reading" (in this case the Assembly Floor). The clerk reads the bill's number, author, and descriptive title. The bill is then sent electronically to the Office of State Printing. A bill must be in print for thirty days, giving time for public review, before it can be acted on. During this time, I compiled my own contact list of acquaintances, friends and family and solicited their help in sending in support letters, and most followed through with their promises.

Fortunately, there were no problems with opposition or protests from any groups or organizations, which meant no obstacles to interrupt the flow.

The bill then went to the Assembly Rules Committee where it was assigned to the appropriate policy committee for its first hearing. As soon as the bill, AB 2517, was assigned to the Judicial Committee, I took the correspondence to the next level. Now we had a target audience in which to lobby for "aye" votes. With a little over thirty days to convince the committee to favorably pass the bill onward, I had to quickly increase my network of supporters. Driving down Pacific Coast Highway in Laguna Beach one afternoon, I suddenly saw Main Beach in a whole new light. Walking up to strangers had worked in the past, giving me experience and confidence to do it again. I quickly parked, grabbed my stack of form letters and started approaching beach goers, my strategy being that this was a public place where people were not in a hurry, full of families with grandparents along who were the best prospects.

The next few weekends were spent at Main Beach, then Corona Del Mar Beach, and finally back to my friends at the Elks Club, where I was handed the microphone during Sunday afternoon social hour. They were such a great group, all eager to sign the support letters.

I now had about two hundred signed form letters that I had to somehow get to the nine committee members before the scheduled hearing. Assemblyman Tran's Costa Mesa District Office kindly accommodated me by allowing me access to their fax machine. I spread the task over three visits just to break up the tedium of feeding some two hundred pages to nine different fax numbers.

Barrett, one of Tran's staff, suggested that I approach the head of a few organizations; this would give me more credibility and recognition, and kill two birds with one stone, by hitting a large group through contact with one person. I took his advice, doing a computer search for California-based grandparent organizations.

I approached the California AARP office in Pasadena, and "persistently" solicited director Ernie Powell for his support of Bill AB 2517. AARP, a very large and powerful non-profit organization for people over the age of 50, had potential to make a huge impact, earning respect and gaining attention. Mr. Powell was impressed with my tenacity, even calling me once to ask, jokingly, "Who are you?" He agreed to offer his assistance, but I had to do the legwork and research, consisting of interpreting and applying AARP'S Public Policy Recommendation on the subject of grandparent visitation. After navigating the site, I zoomed in on the Personal Legal Rights Chapter 12-23, "Legal Rights Of Grandparents." I forwarded my letter, requesting AARP endorsement in the way of a support letter to be sent to the Judicial Committee once it cleared the Sacramento office for approval. I earned his respect, and yes, he was glad to get rid of me. Casey Young, Advocacy manager in Sacramento and Ernie Powell, on May 5, 2006, submitted the golden letter to the committee.

The Honorable Van Tran
California State Assembly
Room 4009
Sacramento, CA95814

Re: AB 2517 (Tran) As introduced — SUPPORT

Dear Assembly Member Tran,

On behalf of over 3 million AARP members in California, I want to express our support for your AB 2517, which ensures grandparents can seek visitation with a grandchild who is adopted by a stepparent.

AARP research has found that grandparent involvement is a vital feature in the growth and well-being of their grandchildren. These relationships become even more important when families are dissolving and changing, so it is important to provide a mechanism to enable a child's relationship with his or her grandparent to continue in these circumstances. This bill recognizes the value of the grandparent relationship and simply allows grandparents to make a reasonable case for visitation when a stepparent adopts the grandchild.

We applaud your leadership on this issue, and look forward to working with you to ensure the enactment of this legislation. If you have any questions concerning our position, or we can be of any assistance, please contact Ernie Powell at epowell@aarp.org or (626) 585-2605.

Respectfully,

CASEY L. YOUNG
Advocacy Manager

cc: Members, Assembly Judiciary Committee
Drew Liebert, Chief Counsel,
Assembly Judiciary Committee
Mark Redmond, Consultant,
Assembly Republican Office of Policy
Tom Porter
Ernie Powell

May 9, 2006 at 9 a.m. was the scheduled hearing date when the author presents the bill and opposition or support is heard and the committee votes on the bill. My speech was written, with airline and hotel reservations confirmed when two days prior to my departure, Jennifer Tannehill called with good news. Apparently, because of unanimous support and zero opposition, the bill had been recommended to be included on the "Proposed Consent Calendar," a file for bills that received no dissenting votes in committee. She explained that this is a very good thing, and only a small percentage of bills, about 25%, are enlisted into this elite section.

Despite the strong possibility that I wouldn't have the opportunity to testify, I kept my original plan and made the trip. My cab dropped me at Amber House, a historical landmark Victorian bed and breakfast, located in a residential tree-lined street. Downtown Sacramento architecture is fascinating, an eclectic mix of 1940's houses, cafes, and the Capitol with its surrounding government buildings. The website advertised the B&B as a short walk to the Capitol, but it was actually more like 15 blocks, and in heels it seemed even farther. Blisters began to form on my feet, and I arrived in a slightly wilted state after padding along in 80 degree heat. The grounds around the Capitol are lovely, lots of well manicured lawns, with a variety of mature shade trees, and a spectacular garden of blooming roses. Once inside, most of it looks like a hospital with painted directional floor tiles and pale grey walls along a maze of corridors. But once you cross over to the rotunda area under the dome, it is rich with warm wood, high ceilings, and soft lighting. The best part is the elevators, with an actual human operator. The dome section is the original building. Its quality materials and design make the newer mismatched building seem sterile by comparison.

I familiarized myself with the layout as Jennifer showed me around the cafeteria, book store and some offices. The following day I would be on my own. I was glad the bill was doing well but disappointed that I wouldn't be able to give my speech. I was prepared and looking forward to standing up for my cause.

Instead, I attended the hearings as an observer, listening as witness representatives from various organizations pled their cases, while oppositional forces rebutted, causing the hearings to drag on. I watched the committee members interact at various stages, sometimes challenging the legislator and the witness. My assignment for the rest of the day was to do a little lobbying for the next phase, by hand-delivering a "fact sheet" about the bill to the potential upcoming committee on the Senate side. This was a good ice breaker for me to walk into the five or so legislators' offices and introduce myself to their staff and talk a little about the bill.

Absent the anticipation and drama of testifying, my trip ended on an upward note with a great big "win." We had successfully overcome our first hurdle.

The second and third readings during the Assembly sessions went smoothly because the bill was now packaged in the "consent" file, bypassing the explanation /discussion requirement during session, and need for individual vote. Once the House of origin approves the bill, it proceeds to the other House where the steps are repeated.

The next month was somewhat less demanding, with most of the legwork behind me. I only had to fax 200 letters to five Senators this time and find constituents in each of their districts to write letters.

Once again, I planned a trip to Sacramento for June 27th and once again it was likely that I would not get to read my speech. Just in case, I traveled there anyway, only just for the day since the hearing was scheduled for 1:30 p.m. At the last minute, it was added to the "consent calendar," eliminating testimony and appearance from the author and witnesses. I should have been happy, and I was, but I wish I could've read my speech. The backup plan was for me to deliver a new "fact sheet" to all forty Senate offices, urging them to vote for the bill during the next session.

Even though the bill passed one House [Assembly] and remained in the "consent" file, it could still be challenged in the other House [Senate], which was why lobbying on behalf of the bill was a good idea. My Pumas got me through this task, covering five floors, up and down stairs, in and out of elevators, and zig-zagging between buildings. Each office was different; sometimes the staff engaged me in conversation about the bill, inviting me to sit and chat, some extremely friendly, others not so much.

July was a holiday month for the Legislature; nothing to do but wait. I opted to stay close to home and baby-sit the bill. Conscientious person that I am, I didn't want to risk the possibility of a potential problem with an oppositional group while I was gone, so I chose to remain close to home, with my phone and computer handy.

August 1 the legislators returned and the bill had to be read two more times during session, remaining on the "consent calendar" before moving on to the Governor.

Jamie Rosales, the new legislative director for Assemblyman Tran, explained that although the bill had been fast-tracked up to this point, the Governor has three choices. He can sign the bill into law, or not sign it and it becomes law without his signature, or veto it.

What could I do to convince the Governor to sign the bill? My last effort to assure the passing of the bill was to write a heartfelt letter to Governor Schwarzenegger. As a back up, I enlisted a friend, who was a supporter of the governor, one of my relatives, and an attorney to also send letters urging his support.

On August 22, I was awakened from a deep sleep at 10:45 p.m. by the ringing of my phone. A man's voice that I didn't recognize was on the other end, asking me questions about the bill; groggily I acknowledged that he had the right person, but I responded snappishly when he accidentally recited the wrong bill number. Convinced it was some sort of crank call, I was in the process of hanging up, when the man corrected his mistake and patiently explained that he was in fact,

Assemblyman Tran. Still not quite believing it was really him, I continued to listen carefully until I recognized his voice. He went on to express his excitement that the bill had been signed hours earlier, and that everyone was working overtime, which is why he called so late. I profusely apologized and expressed my gratitude to him, not sure how my words came out, due to my semi-comatose state.

I followed up with thank you letters to him, his staff, and the Governor, later receiving a phone call of appreciation from the Governor's office.

On January 1, 2007 the bill became law. I had the pleasure to view it in the Standard California Codes six-in-two 2007 edition published by Lexis Nexis four days later, in Attorney Sheryl Edgar's office, as she ceremoniously ripped the plastic cover from the new book.

This is how one ordinary citizen with extraordinary passion came to change a law.

ACTUAL CALIFORNIA STATE LEGISLATIVE DOCUMENTS:

BILL ANALYSIS

Date of Hearing: May 9, 2006

ASSEMBLY COMMITTEE ON JUDICIARY
Dave Jones, Chair
AB 2517 (Tran) - As Introduced: February 23, 2006

PROPOSED CONSENT

SUBJECT:
CHILDREN: GRANDPARENTS' VISITATION RIGHTS

KEY ISSUE:
SHOULD FAMILY COURTS BE PERMITTED TO ALLOW A GRANDPARENT A REASONABLE OPPORTUNITY TO VISIT WITH HIS OR HER GRANDCHILD IN THE LIMITED CIRCUMSTANCE WHEN A STEPPARENT ADOPTS THE GRANDCHILD AND:

1) THE COURT FINDS THERE IS A PREEXISTING RELATIONSHIP BETWEEN THE GRANDPARENT AND THE GRANDCHILD THAT HAS ENGENDERED A BOND SUCH THAT VISITATION IS IN THE BEST INTEREST OF THE CHILD; AND

2) THE COURT BALANCES THE INTEREST OF THE CHILD IN HAVING VISITATION WITH THE GRANDPARENT AGAINST THE RIGHT OF THE PARENTS TO EXERCISE THEIR PARENTAL AUTHORITY?

SYNOPSIS

This non-controversial bill seeks to add stepparent adoptions to the list of circumstances that allow a grandparent to seek visitation with a minor child when the natural or adoptive parents are still married. In support of the bill, various groups including the Family Law Section of the State Bar, the California Alliance for Retired Americans, the Foundation for Grandparenting, and the Grandkidsandme Foundation note how helpful having grandparents in children's lives can be, especially when the trauma of divorce and separation confront the state's families. The existing protections that provide appropriate discretion to family law judges in these instances, including the requirement to balance the interest of the child in having visitation with the grandparent against the right of the parents to exercise their parental authority, are retained in the measure, and there is no known opposition to the bill.

SUMMARY: Seeks to amend the grandparent visitation statute in the Family Code in the limited circumstance when a stepparent adopts the grandchild. Specifically, this bill adds stepparent adoption as one of the limited circumstances when a family court may permit reasonable grandparent visitation with a grandchild while the natural or adoptive parents are married only when the court finds it to be in the grandchild's best interest, and the court (1) finds that there is a preexisting relationship between the grandparent and the grandchild that has engendered a bond such that visitation is in the best interest of the child, and (2) balances the interest of the child in having visitation with the grandparent against the right of the parents to exercise their parental authority.

EXISTING LAW:

1) Authorizes the court to grant reasonable visitation to a grandparent if visitation is found to be in the best interests of the child, and if either parent of a minor is deceased, to the children, siblings, parents, and grandparents of the deceased parent.(Family Code Section 3102 and 3103.)

2) Provides that a grandparent may not file a petition for visitation while the parents are still married unless the parents are living separately on a permanent basis, one of the parents has been absent for more than one month without the other spouse knowing the whereabouts of the other spouse, one of the parents joins in the petition of the grandparents, or the child is not residing with either parent.(Family Code Section 3104(b).)

3) Requires that a court, when considering a grandparent petition for visitation, find that there is a preexisting relationship between the grandparent and the grandchild that has engendered a bond such that visitation is in the best interest of the child. (Family Code Section 3104(a)(1).)

4) Requires that the court, when considering a grandparent petition for visitation, balance the interest of the child in having visitation with the grandparent against the right of the parents to exercise their parental authority. (Family Code Section 3104 (a)(2).)

5) Provides there is a rebuttable presumption that the visitation of a grandparent is not in the best interest of a child if the natural or adoptive parents agree that the grandparents should not be granted visitation rights. (Family Code Section 3104(e).)

FISCAL EFFECT:
This bill is currently keyed non-fiscal.

COMMENTS: This bill seeks to add stepparent

adoptions to the list of circumstances that would allow a grandparent to petition for visitation when a minor child's natural or adoptive parents are still married. In support of the bill, the author states:

It is common knowledge that children who have strong, loving adults in their lives thrive. Grandparents can be that strong, loving adult for a child. These relationships become even more vital during times when families are dissolving and changing? Simply, AB 2517 would allow grandparents to petition the court for visitation of their grandchildren after a stepparent adoption has occurred. This will allow the court to decide if visitation with the grandparent is in the best interest of the child. If so, it will allow grandchild/grandparent relationships to continue when they are needed most.

Legal Backdrop: While "it cannot now be doubted that the Due Process Clause of the Fourteenth Amendment protects the fundamental right of parents to make decisions concerning the care, custody, and control of their children" (Troxel v. Granville, (2000) 530 U. S. 57, 66), grandparents in California have been granted a reasonable and thoughtful statutory right by the Legislature to visit with their grandchild.(See, e.g., White v. Jacobs, (1988) 198 Cal. App. 3d 122, 124-125.)

In California, the Legislature enacted Family Code Section 3104 to permit grandparents to petition the family court for reasonable visitation with their minor grandchildren. The statute was subsequently challenged as being unconstitutional in the case of In re Marriage of Harris. However the California Supreme Court thereafter held that Family Code Section 3104, which this measure seeks to amend, is not unconstitutional.

Unlike the Washington statute at issue in the Troxel case noted above, the Court held that California's so-called grandparent visitation statute, Family Code Section 3104, is narrowly tailored to only allow grandparent visitation, and the rebuttable presumption in the statute against grandparent visitation gives the parent's decision special weight when the court considers whether to grant any visitation with grandparents.

Currently, Family Code Section 3104 only allows grandparents to petition for visitation with their grandchild while the child's natural or adopted parents are still married under limited circumstances that do not yet include the circumstance when a stepparent adopts the grandchild. Presently, a stepparent may adopt a minor child, and thereafter the parental rights of the absent parent are extinguished, the stepparent assumes the parental rights of the absent biological parent, the minor child's natural or adoptive parents are married, and the grandparents are then essentially statutorily barred from seeking visitation. This measure addresses that conundrum, permitting but certainly not requiring a family court to allow for reasonable visitation by the grandparents with the grandchild only when the court finds that there is a preexisting relationship between the grandparent and the grandchild that has engendered a bond such that visitation is in the best interest of the child, and the court balances the interest of the child in having visitation with the grandparent against the right of the parents to exercise their parental authority.

The Lopez Facts This Bill Thoughtfully Addresses: This was the situation in the case of Lopez v. Martinez, (2000) 85 Cal. App. 4th 279. In Lopez, the mother of a child moved in with her parents when the child's father left. The mother lived with the grandparents for several years until she married, at which time she denied the grandparents visitation of the minor child. The grandparents petitioned for visitation of the child under Family Code Section 3104, citing the child's father's whereabouts were unknown to meet the circumstances required to seek visitation. During that time, however, the child's stepfather adopted the child, and the mother moved to dissolve the visitation order.

The Court of Appeal found that the adoption by the stepfather created a change in circumstance that required the court to dissolve the visitation order. The stepfather was legally considered the child's adopted father and was married to the child's mother. As none of the other circumstances were present under Family Code Section 3104, under the plain language of the statute the court had to dissolve the visitation order at the parent's request.

It is important to note that this measure, while adding stepparent adoption to the list of circumstances that would allow grandparents to petition the court for visitation of their minor grandchildren, it would not change the amount of deference the court gives the parent's decision to deny visitation to grandparents. Nor does it appear to alter the rights of parents, or adoptive stepparents, in any way, but instead merely adjusts the conditions necessary to seek reasonable grandparent visitation rights.

ARGUMENTS IN SUPPORT:
In support of the bill, the Family Law Section of the State Bar (Flexcom) writes that:

The addition of 3104(b)(5) establishes a limited class of grandparents, which have standing to request grandparent visitation. It is important to note that the protections in place in the statute provide that the petitioning grandparents "must" have an established relationship with the grandchild and also that there remains the "presumption" that grandparent visitation is not in the best interest of the grandchild, if both parents in an intact marriage object to said visitation request. Although grandparent visitation litigation is expensive and many times initiated or opposed in bad faith, children cannot have too many grandparents, if those grandparent relationships are determined to be in their best interest.

The California Alliance for Retired Americans writes in support that "We believe that the support of grandparents for their grandchildren is in the best interests of the child(ren) especially during a time of crisis such as a divorce."

The Foundation for Grandparenting also writes in support that research outlines the critical nature of the grandparent-grandchild relationship and how facilitating this relationship benefits all generations. In addition, the Grandkidsandme Foundation writes in support that:

There is no single answer for dealing with your adult children and grandchildren's pain during the time of divorce. Each family must discover its own path, but concern, empathy and love displayed in a variety of ways by both the parents and grandparents are important? If grandparents can remain neutral in their involvement, they will be in a better position to assist their children and grandchildren? During this critical time, a grandparent needs to be a model of unconditional love for the parents and the grandchildren.

REGISTERED SUPPORT / OPPOSITION:

Support

Family Law Section of the California State Bar (Flexcom)
CA Alliance for Retired Americans
The Foundation for Grandparenting
The Grandkidsandme Foundation
Many individuals

Opposition: None on file

Analysis Prepared by: Drew Liebert and Amanda Kirchner / JUD / (916) 319-2334

BILL ANALYSIS

SENATE JUDICIARY COMMITTEE
Senator Joseph L. Dunn, Chair
2005-2006 Regular Session
AB 2517A
Assembly Member Tran
As Introduced
Hearing Date: June 27, 20062
Family Code 5
BCP:rm1
7

SUBJECT

Minor Children: Visitation Rights

DESCRIPTION

This bill would allow a grandparent to petition the court for visitation with their grandchild when the natural or adoptive parents are married, and the grandchild has been adopted by a stepparent.

BACKGROUND

It has long been recognized that the "Due Process Clause of the Fourteenth Amendment protects the fundamental right of parents to make decisions concerning the care, custody, and control of their children."[Troxel v. Granville (2000) 530 U. S. 57, 66.] In order to accommodate grandparents who wish to petition for visitation rights to their grandchildren, the Legislature enacted SB 306 (Lockyer). That bill sought to balance a grandparent's ability to petition for visitation rights against the parent's right to make decisions about the care, custody and control of their children. The statute was subsequently upheld by the California Supreme Court as not violating the parent's fundamental right over the custody, care and control over their children. [In re Marriage of Harris (2004) 34 Cal. 4th 210, 230.]

Currently, grandparents are restricted in their ability to petition for visitation of their grandchildren when the natural or adoptive parents are married, unless one of several circumstances exists. AB 2517 would additionally authorize petitions for visitation when the "child has been adopted by a stepparent."That change would further facilitate grandparent visitation in cases where the family has become divided over the years, and remove the possibility of a stepparent preventing visitation with the child by adopting that child.

CHANGES TO EXISTING LAW

Existing law allows a court to grant reasonable visitation to a grandparent if the court determines that visitation is in the best interests of the child. [Fam. Code3103.]

Existing law requires a court, prior to granting visitation, to find a preexisting relationship with the grandparent such that visitation is in the best interests of the child, and balance the interest of the child in having visitation against the parent's rights. [Fam. Code 3104(a).]

Existing law prevents grandparents from petitioning for visitation while the natural or adoptive parents are married, unless: the parents are currently living separately and apart on a permanent or indefinite basis; one or more of the parents has been absent for more than one month without the other spouse knowing the whereabouts of the absent spouse; one of the parents joins in the petition with the grandparents; or the child is not residing with either parent. [Fam. Code 3104.]

This bill would add when a "child has been adopted by a stepparent" to the above list of circumstances where a grandparent can file a petition for visitation.

COMMENT

1. Stated need for the bill

According to the author, and numerous supporters,

[This bill] would allow grandparents to petition the court for visitation of their grandchild, after their grandchild has been adopted by a new stepparent. The grandparent/grandchild relationship is one that is especially vital to retain in today's changing families.

Often families are ripped apart through divorce or other negative circumstances. Solid relationships that children could once count on, are then in doubt and become less stable. Stability can come through maintaining strong grandparent/grandchild relationships through those family changes.

Grandparents often play many roles in a family. They offer emotional support and comfort, relay family history, and give advice.

. . .

Simply, AB 2517 would allow grandparents to petition the court for visitation of their grandchildren after a stepparent adoption has occurred. This will allow the court to decide if visitation with the grandparent is in the best interest of the child. If so, it will allow the grandchild/ grandparent relationships to continue where they are needed most.

2. PROPOSED CHANGE WOULD ALTER THE OUTCOME OF LOPEZ V. MARTINEZ

In Lopez v. Martinez (2005) 85 Cal. App. 4th 279, the court terminated the grandparents' visitation with their grandchild after the stepparent adoption of that child. That decision was based on their interpretation of current Family Code statutes restricting the situations were a grandparent can petition for visitation with their grandchild.

Specially, if the natural or adoptive parents of the grandchild are married, a grandparent can only petition under certain limited circumstances. Moreover, if those limited circumstances cease to exist, the parent or parents can petition the court to terminate grandparent visitation. The court is required to grant that petition.[Fam. Code3104.]

In Lopez, the grandparents raised their grandchild for four and a half years in their home with his mother. The mother subsequently married and moved with her child to into another residence with her husband. The grandparents subsequently petitioned for visitation based on the provision that allows such visitation when "[o]ne of the parents has been absent for more than one month without the other spouse knowing the whereabouts of the absent spouse." [Fam. Code3104(a)(3).]The court granted that petition after finding the requisite relationship between the grandparents and grandchild, and balancing the interest of the child in visitation against the right of the parents to exercise their authority over the child. Subsequently, the mother's new husband adopted the grandchild, and the mother petitioned the court to terminate the grand-parent's visitation due to the change in circum-stances. The trial court found that the adoption did not constitute changed circumstances warranting termination of visitation, but the appellate court disagreed. [85 Cal. App 4th at 288-89.]

The Court of Appeal's decision was based on a literal reading of the statute that limits grandparents' peti-tions for visitation when the natural or adoptive parents of a child are married.[Fam. Code3104(b).] Once the child was adopted by the stepparent, that individual became the child's parent. Thus, the basis for the grandparent's visitation under the statute, that one parent was absent, was removed. In making its decision, the Court of Appeal noted that "this may be one of those relatively rare cases where adher-ence to a statutory rule may work an injustice in the particular case." [85 Cal. App. 4th at 288.]

Accordingly, AB 2517 seeks to address this situation by specifically adding when a "child has been adopted by a stepparent" to the list of situations where a grandparent can petition for visitation with their grandchildren. This addition removes the ability for a stepparent to adopt that child to prevent a grandparent otherwise found to qualify for visitation, from having that visitation.

3. Lack of constitutional problems with the proposed language. Previous challenges to Family Code Section 3104 were based on the fundamental right of a parent to the care, custody and control of their children. [Troxel v. Granville (2000) 530 U. S. 57, 66; In re Marriage of Harris (2004) 34 Cal. 4th 210, 230.]This section previously withstood Constitutional scrutiny due to its required balancing of interests, and rebuttable presumption against grandparent visitation under certain circumstances where the natural or adoptive parent objects. [In re Marriage of Harris (2004), 34 Cal. 4th at 226-30.]

AB 2517 would not modify either the required court findings, balancing of interests, or the rebuttable presumption. Thus, although this will allow grandparent visitation in certain circumstances not currently allowed, this visitation does not violate a parent's fundamental rights regarding their children. Support: Family Law Section of the State Bar; Marian Bergeson, Former State Senator, AARP; California Alliance for Retired Americans; Foundation for Grandparenting; Grandkidsandme Foundation; 175 individuals

Opposition: None Known

HISTORY

Source: Author

Related Pending Legislation: None Known
Prior Legislation:SB 1406 (Kuehl, 2002), would have revised provisions relating to child custody mediators. (This bill died in Senate Rules.)

SB 174 (Kuehl, Chapter 1077, Statutes of 2002), authorized the voluntarily adoption of a confidential mediation program that would prohibit the mediator from making a recommendation as to custody or visitation to anyone other than the disputing parties, except as specified.

AB 2209 (Honda, 1998), would have revised provision relating to stepparent and grandparent visitation.(This was never heard.)

Prior Vote:Asm. Floor (Ayes 79, Noes 0)
Asm. Jud. (Ayes 9, Noes 0)

****

BILL NUMBER: AB 2517
CHAPTERED
BILL TEXT

CHAPTER138
FILED WITH SECRETARY OF STATE AUGUST 22, 2006
APPROVED BY GOVERNOR AUGUST 22, 2006
PASSED THE SENATE AUGUST 10, 2006
PASSED THE ASSEMBLY MAY 15, 2006

INTRODUCED BY Assembly Member Tran

FEBRUARY 23, 2006
An act to amend Section 3104 of the Family Code, relating to minor children.

LEGISLATIVE COUNSEL'S DIGEST

AB 2517, Tran Minor children: visitation rights.

Existing law authorizes the court, on petition by a grandparent of a minor child, to grant reasonable visitation rights to the grandparent if the court both finds that there is a preexisting relationship between the grandparent and grandchild, as specified, such that visitation is in the child's best interest, and the court balances the interest of the child in having visitation with the grandparent against the rights of parents to exercise their parental authority.

Existing law further prohibits a petition for visitation from being filed while the natural or adoptive parents are married, unless the parents are currently living separately and apart, one parent has been absent for more than one month without the other spouse knowing the whereabouts of the absent spouse, one of the parents joins in the petition with the grandparents, or the child is not residing with either parent.

This bill would also authorize a petition for visitation to be filed when the child has been adopted by a stepparent.

THE PEOPLE OF THE STATE OF CALIFORNIA DO ENACT AS FOLLOWS:

SECTION 1.
Section 3104 of the Family Code is amended to read:

3104.(a) On petition to the court by a grandparent of a minor child, the court may grant reasonable visitation rights to the grandparent if the court does both of the following:

(1) Finds that there is a preexisting relationship between the grandparent and the grandchild that has engendered a bond such that visitation is in the best interest of the child.

(2) Balances the interest of the child in having visitation with the grandparent against the right of the parents to exercise their parental authority.

(b) A petition for visitation under this section may not be filed while the natural or adoptive parents are married, unless one or more of the following circumstances exist:

(1) The parents are currently living separately and apart on a permanent or indefinite basis.

(2) One of the parents has been absent for more than one month without the other spouse knowing the whereabouts of the absent spouse.

(3) One of the parents joins in the petition with the

grandparents.

(4) The child is not residing with either parent.

(5) The child has been adopted by a stepparent.

At any time that a change of circumstances occurs such that none of these circumstances exist, the parent or parents may move the court to terminate grandparental visitation and the court shall grant the termination.

(c) The petitioner shall give notice of the petition to each of the parents of the child, any stepparent, and any person who has physical custody of the child, by personal service pursuant to Section 415.10 of the Code of Civil Procedure.

(d) If a protective order as defined in Section 6218 has been directed to the grandparent during the pendency of the proceeding, the court shall consider whether the best interest of the child requires that any visitation by that grandparent should be denied.

(e) There is a rebuttable presumption that the visitation of a grandparent is not in the best interest of a minor child if the natural or adoptive parents agree that the grandparent should not be granted visitation rights.

(f) There is a rebuttable presumption affecting the burden of proof that the visitation of a grandparent is not in the best interest of a minor child if the parent who has been awarded sole legal and physical custody of the child in another proceeding, or the parent with whom the child resides if there is currently no operative custody order objects to visitation by the grandparent.

(g) Visitation rights may not be ordered under this section if that would conflict with a right of custody or visitation of a birth parent who is not a party to the proceeding.

(h) Visitation ordered pursuant to this section shall not create a basis for or against a change of residence of the child, but shall be one of the factors for the court to consider in ordering a change of residence.

(i) When a court orders grandparental visitation pursuant to this section, the court in its discretion may, based upon the relevant circumstances of the case:

(1) Allocate the percentage of grandparental visitation between the parents for purposes of the calculation of child support pursuant to the statewide uniform guideline (Article 2 (commencing with Section 4050) of Chapter 2 of Part 2 of Division 9).

(2) Notwithstanding Sections 3930 and 3951, order a parent or grandparent to pay to the other, an amount for the support of the child or grandchild. For purposes of this paragraph, "support" means costs related to visitation such as any of the following:
(A) Transportation.

(B) Provision of basic expenses for the child or grandchild, such as medical expenses, day care costs, and other necessities.

(j) As used in this section, "birth parent" means "birth parent" as defined in Section 8512.

Our grandchildren accept us for ourselves, without rebuke or effort to change us, as no one in our entire lives has ever done, not our parents, siblings, spouses, friends-and hardly ever our own grown children.

-ruth goode

Seven

Grandparent Rights: Standing Up For a Child

It is referred to as grandparent rights, but in reality it is the rights of children to remain connected with grandparents. The grandparent visitation rights movement is directed toward protecting and preserving that part of a child's extended family. The grandparents' rights movement is an ongoing struggle of individuals promoting the preservation of the family unit by influencing legislation and the public.

Advocates include organizations, legal and therapeutic professionals, and concerned citizens. Grandparent rights give grandparents standing in a court of law, which means they may petition the court for visitation with a grandchild when they find themselves entangled with visitation issues. Most often the problem arises when the strained relationship with one or both parents escalates and after exhausting all efforts to rectify the denied visitation issue, grandparents resort to litigation.

The idea of seeking litigation as a means to visit a grandchild is indeed a strange phenomenon, yet a fact of life as it is today. Family values have changed; the Baby Boomer Generation, now grandparents, find that their children, as parents, often have a different set of family values. Dr. Carson's quote, from her book, "The Essential Grandparent," explains it best. "Unfortunately, it seems very likely that the nuclear family is not a viable social form. It is too small. Each person in a nuclear family is too tightly linked to other members of the family; any one relationship that goes sour, even for a few hours, becomes critical; people cannot simply turn away from grandparents, grandchildren, aunts, uncles, cousins, brothers."

These children, who are now parents, so hastily dispose of the grandparents, seemingly whenever the mood strikes them. Communication efforts become broken, and there is little if any dialogue or consideration toward mediation, consequently the consensus of the parent[s] is to get rid of the person, rather than the problem.

Researchers found that adults who have strong relationships with grandparents tend to be much more positive about the importance and value of older citizens. This being said, there is now an evolution in the family in contemporary society, from extended to nuclear. It is the barrier that is created by the nuclear family structure that isolates them from a more extended kinship connection with, for example, grandparents.

The grandparents interviewed concluded that they observed a characteristic sense of entitlement and selfishness in their children. Our rationale is that we probably did too much and gave too much, thereby creating spoiled children. We wanted them to have more than we had growing up, so perhaps we share responsibility for the societal shift in family values. There are a variety of explanations that contribute to the denial of access: divorce, presence of a new partner, death of one of the parents, drug abuse, economic issues, and mental illness is a possible factor. There are situations where symptoms of borderline personality disorder present themselves in one of the parents, creating an even more complicated obstacle for visitation. The frustrating part is there is no reasoning with an unreasonable person who refuses to get help. In one study, a certain pattern emerged, which was that mostly ex-daughters-in-law initiated the denial against the paternal grandparent.

Whatever the reason for the disrespect and dishonor of the elder generation, grandparents find themselves in a position of instability and a state of uncertainty; their role in the family is suddenly threatened and soon to be extinguished. They begin to feel insignificant. The children at the center of this tug of war are equally disrespected by parents because their best interests are discounted: it is as if they are being treated like pieces of property. Grandparents realize this and move into protective mode.

Once the initial shock dissipates, the grandparents begin looking for answers, sometimes in the form of support and advice and sometimes they require legal information. They are desperate to re-connect with their grandchildren and they don't have a set of guidelines preparing them for the parental negotiating they may have to do, nor do they understand their legal rights. They want to lend a voice to the child and stand up for them as well as for themselves.

Grandparent visitation laws are not uniform, each

state is different, and they can be complicated and confusing, leaving it up to individual judges for interpretation. Nothing is ironclad and the laws are always undergoing revisions. As long as grandparent rights laws are in a state of flux and the parents involved fail to recognize the value of the grandparent-grandchild relationship, then grandparents must do whatever is necessary to keep the peace.

When grandparents seek my advice about the broken relationships between family, and their lost grandchild access, I pass on the words of wisdom a very wise person, Rick Harrison, M. A., MFT, shared with me over and over. He explained, using many examples of the benefits of the "you and me" approach to communication, rather than the "you or me" [one against the other], taking the least adversarial path is always best if possible. The goal here is to re-connect with the parents as a means to maintain the relationship with the grandchild. The parents are the ones that have all of the power over the grandchildren.

Re-connecting with the parent[s] is just that; it's all about them, not the grandkids. Make a sincere effort to make them feel important by telling them, by showing them, by spending time with them, sending a small thoughtful gift, like a coffee card. Parents often feel that they are indeed the common enemy between grandparent and child.

Grandparents might first want to abandon their ego. Does it really matter who's right? Give up that need to be right, if you want to see the child. Do whatever it takes to mend fences. You are in the fight of your life to remain connected to your grandchild, so gather every bit of your strength and strategize intelligently. Be smart, resourceful, and keep emotions in check. If the parent[s] want to engage in the blame and shame game, so be it, don't defend yourself; this is about their issues. You know the truth about yourself and that's all that matters. Your opinion is what counts, not theirs. Don't take it personally.

Grandparents want to take the highest road possible; you want to be the diplomat, listen, keep quiet, and empathize. People want to be heard, so listen and let them realize that you comprehend. You are not agreeing that they are right and you are wrong, but just by listening you are acknowledging that you hear what they are saying and that you understand their feelings. That's it!

Grandparents very well may disagree with the parents' rules and philosophy, so disagree in silence. Keep your advice to yourself. Parents have the power. For the sake of the child, it is better to bite one's tongue and go along with the program. Lower expectations, and accept whatever the parents are willing to give you, even if it's monitored visitation. At this point, I would take as little as five minutes a year just for a chance to hug my grandson. Grandparents can ill afford to rock the boat. Walk on eggshells if necessary. Remain focused. Remember the prize.

It has been established that children need grandparents in their lives as an emotional balance to healthy development. Dr. Carson emphasized that it is the grandparents' efforts that meet the child's needs, giving them strength not just to endure but to prosper. Grandparents as they age, thrive knowing they have a strong generational bond with grandchildren and a desire to protect lineage. These needs and wants are reciprocal, which guides the ship of activism. Grandparents are the only ones that can advocate for themselves and the child, and offer up that much needed voice.

When all attempts at reconciliation have failed, litigation is the next step. The process is stressful, costly, time consuming and the delays in the system are frustrating. Obtaining a court ordered visitation document so you can see your grandchild is well worth the effort and inconvenience. Children absolutely need continued contact with grandparents.

Grandparents would do well to familiarize themselves with their individual state statutes that comprise grandparent rights. The Internet is a valuable resource; navigate to the official state site or go to Findlaw.com or Divorcesource.com, where it is more user-friendly. Public libraries and state legislators are there to provide information to the citizens of the community they serve. It is important to keep yourself informed and perform due diligence.

When the red flags start flying and it becomes evident that conflict is brewing, that is the time to begin a journal. Keep a log of dates and times of every conversation, every broken promise, save letters and e-mail between you and the parent[s]. Write down everything and document all prior visits with the child. Log in every attempt and request to have a visit. Take many photos of you with the child; this is very important to establish a pre-existing relationship.

The most crucial deciding factor before seeking legal action is an ethical issue. What effects will litigation have on the child? Will the child suffer, feel sad and hurt? Will the pursuit of justice destabilize the home environment? Will the child be thrust in the middle of a war between grandparents and parents to the degree that he or she becomes uncomfortable at the thought of seeing the grandparent? The child may become fearful of losing the parents' love and feel conflict. They may feel disloyal toward the parents if they express a desire to see the grandparent[s]. In other words, will the child's life be filled with turmoil because of the threat of legal action brought upon the parent by the grandparent? If the child is living with an angry, volatile parent[s] with a history of vindictiveness, then attorney involvement could be like lighting the fuse to a future explosion, thus, putting the child in harm's way. With all of these issues to consider, it may not be worthwhile to proceed at the child's expense. Surrendering and stepping aside may be the only option. We grandparents have an overwhelming instinct to protect and watch over these grandchildren of ours; we feel it is our responsibility. After all, we are second only to a parent. Maybe we can't always protect them.

There is no pain free solution; someone loses no matter the decision. If grandparents prevail and obtain a court ordered visitation agreement, then parents are disappointed and may thwart the facilitation of the order and or begin alienation tactics against the grandparent. If grandparents choose not to exercise their rights, then both the child and grandparent lose future contact. If the child is young and does not understand the reason for the grandparent's disappearance, the child may feel abandoned and unloved by the grandparent for not finding them or persevering in the beginning. Patricia Slorah, Ph. D in her book, "Grandparents' Rights," cites an example of care-giving(highly involved and primary) grandparents, and how emotional abuse is likely to occur when grandparents are separated from grandchildren with whom they have previously had a loving relationship. "The grandchildren believe they are somehow at fault, that their grandparents abandoned them because they are 'bad.' Several grandparents related that upon seeing their grandchild for the first time after obtaining court-ordered visitation, the first thing the child said, was 'please let me come home. I'll be good.'" Dr. Slorah emphasized, "These grandparents were awarded visitation because they convinced the court that their grandchild needed their continuing presence as a stabilizing influence." No matter the circumstances, when the child is suddenly denied access, it is a traumatic experience for them. Grandparents must remain focused on their child-directed purpose; that is the guiding light during uncertain times. To once again quote Dr. Carson: "If you give up your efforts and drift away, your children lose a vital connection, and so do you."

When we lose contact with our grandchildren, we lose a large part of our future. The child not only also loses a piece of their future, but the connection to their past.

Grandparents may have to prove their value to society in order to have the respect bestowed upon them that they deserve. Are grandparents moving toward the direction of becoming insignificant? Or extinction?

It is time for grandparents to become empowered advocates for the welfare of the children and the preservation of the relationship between the two generations. Believe deeply that you matter as a grandparent in a child's life and that your grandchild will prosper because of this deeply vital connection. Maintain a sustained faith in the value of this relationship. It is time for grandparents to become activists on behalf of our future generations. It is time to stand up and fight for a child's liberty interests. It is time to eliminate unreasonable denied access. Build a united front through numbers; join other grandparents to promote change. Contact state representatives and make them aware of the problem in their community. Get informed and share the information with others. Don't ever give up on a child.

Factors Considered for Grandparent Visitation

Grandparents in every state have rights for court mandated visitation orders as a means to see their grandchildren. Recognition of grandparents' rights by state legislatures is a recent manifestation, only in effect for a little over 30 years.

The courts grant visitation to grandparents based on criteria determined by each state's statutes. While the specific conditions differ, every jurisdiction considers the "best interests of the child" as a standard and primary concern when granting visitation.

The following is a list of some of the factors determining the best interests of the child by the court:

1. The wishes of the parent[s] and grandparent[s].

2. The strength of relationship and bond between the grandparent[s] and child.

3. The safety, welfare and needs of the child, physically and emotionally.

4. The length of the relationship between grandparent[s] and child.

5. The capability of the parent[s] or grandparent[s] to meet the needs of the child.

6. Any evidence of substance abuse by the parent[s] or grandparent[s].

7. Effects on the child when grandparents receive

visitation against the wishes of the parent[s].

8. Grandparent[s] must prove the parent is unfit, unreasonable or that the child would suffer without the visitation.

The provisions for visitation in each of the state's laws are constantly revised; constitutionality continues to be an ongoing question often raised within the courts. Provisions, determined to be unconstitutional either in the state supreme court or the U. S. Supreme Court, are not included in the following summary of current state provisions.

From State To Shining State

Alabama: Conditions for the grandparent visitation rights include a determination of whether a parent is deceased, the child's parents are divorced, or the grandparent has been unreasonably denied visitation.
Natural grandparents may have post-adoption visitation when the child is adopted by a stepparent, or other family members. 30-3-4

Alaska: Determination of grandparent visitation rights must be made in an action for divorce, and the best interest of the child. Adoption cuts off the visitation unless the adoption decree specifically provided for visitation between the adopted child and the natural relatives. 25.24.150

Arizona: The child's parents' marriage must have been dissolved for a minimum of three months, or the child is born out of wedlock, parent deceased or missing.

Adoption cuts off visitation rights to the grandparents unless the adoption is to a stepparent. 25-337.01

ARKANSAS: The conditions for grandparent visitation are the child's parents are divorced, the child is in the custody of someone other than the parents, the child resided with the grandparent, or the child is born out of wedlock. Adoption cuts off all visitation rights of the natural grandparents unless the grandparent intervenes in the adoption. 19-13-103

CALIFORNIA: Conditions for grandparent visitation includes, the child's parents are divorced or separated, one parent's whereabouts are unknown, the child is not residing with either parent, one parent is deceased. Grandparents must have had a preexisting relationship with the grandchild. The court must balance visitation with the parents' rights. One parent must join with the grandparent. If both parents agree that the court should not grant visitation, there is a rebuttable presumption that visitation is not in the child's best interests. Natural grandparents may still get visitation. Adoption does not automatically cut off, natural grandparents may still get visitation. 3100-3105

COLORADO: Visitation is granted when the parents' marriage is terminated, legal custody of the child has been given to a third party, the child has been placed outside the home of either of the child's parents, or one of the parent's is deceased. Adoption cuts off unless it is granted to a stepparent.19-1-117

CONNECTICUT: A Court may award visitation if it is in the best interests of the child. Adoption does not automatically cut off the visitation rights of a grandparent. 46b-59

DELAWARE: Best interest of the child. Adoption terminates all rights. 13-72B

FLORIDA: At least one of the child's parents is deceased, marriage of the child's parents is dissolved, a parent has deserted the child, or the child is born out of wedlock and not later determined to be a child born in wedlock. Adoption terminates all rights, except by a stepparent. 752.01

GEORGIA: A Grandparent may intervene during an action when there is questions concerning custody of a minor child, parents' divorce, termination of parental rights, or visitation rights is before the court, or if there has been a stepparent or blood relative adoption. 19-9-3

HAWAII: The court may award visitation to a grandparent, during divorce, separation, annulment, separate maintenance, or any other proceeding where there is at issue a dispute as to the custody of a minor child, unless it is shown that it's not in the child's best interest. Adoption terminates all rights. 571-46-2

IDAHO: Visitation may be granted when the grandparent has established a substantial relationship with the child. Adoption terminates all rights. 32-1008

ILLINOIS: Visitation may be granted if one of the parents is deceased, if either the parents are not cohabitating on a permanent basis, one of the parents has been absent from the home for over one month or whereabouts unknown, one of the parents joins in the petition with the grandparents or great-grandparents, or if a sibling is in state custody. Adoption terminates visitation rights, unless by a stepparent. 750-5/607

INDIANA: A court may award visitation rights if either parent is deceased, child is born out of wedlock, the marriage dissolved in Indiana. Adoption cuts off the visitation rights of the grandparents unless the adoption is by a stepparent or other biologically related family member. 31-1-11.7-1

IOWA: Visitation may be awarded during pending or final divorce of the marriage, the parent who is the child of the petitioning grandparents is deceased, the child has been placed in foster home, the petitioning grandparents are the parents of the non-custodial parent and the other parent's spouse has adopted the child, or the grandparent is the parent of the child's non-custodial parent and the child is born out of wedlock. Adoption by a stepparent does not terminate rights. 598.35

KANSAS: A court may award visitation rights in a custody order. Adoption cuts off the visitation rights of the grandparents unless the grandparent is the parent of a deceased parent and the surviving parent's spouse adopts the child. 60-1616

KENTUCKY: Visitation may be granted if the court determines it is in the best interest of the child.
Visitation rights terminate during adoption, unless by a stepparent and where there has been no termination of the parental rights of the parent whose parents are seeking visitation. 405.021

LOUISIANA: Visitation may be granted to the grandparent, who is the parent of a deceased parent or parent who has been declared legally incompetent and visitation is in the best interest of the child. Adoption cuts off the visitation rights of grandparents except where the grandparents are the parents of a deceased party to the marriage or the parents of a party who no longer has rights to object to the child's adoption. 9.344, Ch. C.1264

MAINE: Visitation may be granted if one of the child's parents is deceased, and it is in the best interest of the child, does not interfere with the parent child relationship and there is a pre-existing relationship with the grandparent. Adoption terminates all rights. 19 M. R. S. A. 1001

MARYLAND: A court may award grandparent visitation if it is in the best interest of the child. Adoption cuts off all visitation rights of the grandparent. 9-102

MASSACHUSETTS: A court may award visitation rights if the child's parents are divorced, separated, one of the parents is deceased, or the child was born out of wedlock with established paternity. Adoption cuts off, unless the adoption is by a stepparent. 119, 36D

MICHIGAN: Visitation can be granted to a grandparent if the child's parents is dissolved, the parents are separated, or custody of the child is given to a third party other than the child's parents. Adoption terminates visitation rights unless by a stepparent. 25.312, 722.27b

MINNESOTA: Visitation rights may be granted if the child's parent is deceased and the grandparents are the parents of the deceased parent; during or after dissolution of marriage, custody, separation, annulment; or if the child resided with the grandparent or great-grandparent for twelve or more months and is subsequently remove by the child's parents. Visitation terminates upon adoption, unless by a stepparent. 257.022

MISSISSIPPI: Visitation rights may be granted to the parents of a non-custodial parent resulting from a proceeding in Mississippi, to the parents of a parent whose parental rights have been terminated, or to a parent of a parent who is deceased. If the court finds that the grandparent of the child has established a strong relationship with the child and the parent has unreasonably denied the grandparent visitation and that it would be in the best interest of the child, any grandparent can file. Adoption cuts off visitation, except to a stepparent or blood relative. 93-16-1

MISSOURI: Visitation rights may be granted if the child's parents have filed for divorce, one parent is deceased and the other parent has unreasonably denied visitation to the grandparent, or when a parent or parents unreasonably deny visitation to a grandparent for more than 90 days. Visitation may terminate following an adoption unless by a stepparent or other blood relative. 452.402

MONTANA: Visitation may be granted when the court finds visitation is in the best interest of the child. Visitation rights terminate on adoption by anyone other than a stepparent or a grandparent. 40-9-101

NEBRASKA: Visitation may be granted if at least one parent is deceased, the parents' marriage has been dissolved or a petition for dissolution has been filed, or the child is born out of wedlock and paternity has been established. Grandparents must demonstrate that a beneficial relationship exists between themselves and the grandchild and that visitation is in the best interest of the child. Visitation cannot interfere with the parent-child relationship. Adoption terminates all rights. 43-1801

NEVADA: If the child's parents are separated or divorced or if one parent is deceased or has relinquished his parental rights or had them terminated, the grandparents and great-grandparents may get visitation if it is in the child's best interest. Specific factors determine best interest. Grandparents may request visitation prior to termination of parental rights. 125A.300

NEW HAMPSHIRE: Visitation may be granted if the child's parents are divorced, or have filed for divorce, one of the parents is deceased, one of the parents has had his or her parental rights terminated, or the child is born out of wedlock, and if visitation is in the best interest of the child. All rights terminate following adoption. 458.17-d

NEW JERSEY: Visitation may be granted if it is in the child's best interest, considering the relationship between grandparent and child, grandparent and parent relationship, time elapsed since last contact, effect the visitation will have on relationship of parent and grandparent, whether parents are divorced, good faith of grandparent and grandparent's history. Adoption terminates visitation except from a stepparent. 9:2-7.1

NEW MEXICO: Visitation may be granted if the child's parents are divorced, separated, or deceased, if the child resided with the grandparent for at least 3 months and was less than 6 years old at the beginning of the 3 month period and was subsequently removed from grandparent's home, [if the child is under 6, the residence requirement is reduced to three months]. Grandparents may obtain visitation after adoption by a stepparent, a relative, guardian appointed by deceased parent, a sponsor, recognized through baptism, confirmation. 40-9-1

NEW YORK: Visitation may be granted if one of the child's parents is deceased or where circumstances show that conditions exist which equity would see fit to intervene. Best interest of the child. Adoption does not automatically cut off. 72.

NORTH CAROLINA: Visitation may be granted as part of any order determining custody of the child, also best interest. Adoption terminates visitation unless by a stepparent or relative of the child where substantial relationship exists between grandparent and the child. 50-13.2

NORTH DAKOTA: Visitation may be granted if the court finds it is in the best interest of the child and would not interfere with the parent-child relationship. Visitation rights terminate unless the adoption is by the stepparent. 14-09-06

OHIO: Visitation may be granted as a part of or subsequent to the parents' divorce, dissolution of marriage, separation, annulment, or child support proceeding if grandparent has an interest in welfare of child and visitation is in the best interest; also included is child born out of wedlock and one of the parents is deceased. Visitation terminates unless by a stepparent. 3109.051, 3109.11

OKLAHOMA: Visitation is granted if it is in the child's best interest. The statute provides special and specific rules if the child is born out of wedlock. Grandparents must show pre-existing relationship with the child. Existing visitation orders do not terminate upon adoption as long as in the best interest of the child. 10 O. S. A. 5

OREGON: Visitation may be granted when there has been a pre-existing relationship between child and grandparent and the grandparent has been denied reasonable contact. Adoption terminates visitation. 109.121

PENNSYLVANIA: Visitation may be granted if one of the child's parents is deceased, the parents are divorced or separated for more than 6 months, or the child has lived with the grandparent more than 12 months. The court must find the visitation to be the best interest of the child and will not interfere with the parent-child relationship, and consider the contact between the grandparent and grandchild. Adoption terminates visitation unless by a stepparent. 23.5311

RHODE ISLAND: Determination of grandparent visitation must include that it is in the best interest if the grandparent is fit, that the grandparent has repeatedly attempted to visit the grandchild during the 12 months preceding the filing of the application and was not allowed to visit as a direct result of the actions of either or both of the parents, and there is no other way the grandparent is able to visit the child, and the grandparent by clear and convincing evidence has successfully rebutted the presumption that the parent's decision to refuse the grandparent visitation was reasonable. Visitation may also be granted if one of the parent's is deceased, or parents are divorced. Adoption terminates all rights. 15-5-24

SOUTH CAROLINA: The court must consider the relationship between the grandparent and the child, divorce, separation and death of one of the parents are determining factors. Adoption terminates all rights. 20-7420

SOUTH DAKOTA: Visitation may be granted if parents are divorced, separated, one parent is deceased. Adoption terminates rights unless by a stepparent or grandparent. 25-4-45

TENNESSEE: Visitation may be granted if the court finds it to be in the child's best interest. Adoption terminates rights unless by a stepparent or other relative of the child. 36-6-301

TEXAS: Conditions for grandparent visitation rights include that one of the parents is deceased, incompetent, incarcerated or nis or her rights terminated. Visitation may also be granted if the parents are divorced,, the child has been abused or neglected, the child has been adjudicated a delinquent, or in need of supervision, the child has lived with the grandparent 6 months within the 24 month period preceding the filing. Adoption terminates rights. 14.03

UTAH: Visitation may be granted if a parent is deceased, or if the child's parents are divorced or separated and must also be in the best interests of the child. Adoption terminates rights. 30-5-1

VERMONT: Conditions for grandparent visitation rights include whether the parent is deceased, incompetent, or if the child has been abandoned, and must be in the

child's best interest. Adoption terminates rights unless adopted by a stepparent or relative of the child. 15.1011
VIRGINIA: Determination of grandparent visitation is made during a suit for dissolution of the child's parents, and must be in the best interests of the child. Adoption terminates rights. 20-124.1

WASHINGTON: Visitation may be granted when it is in the best interests of the child. Adoption terminates rights. 26.09.230

WEST VIRGINIA: Grandparents may be granted visitation during a divorce, separation, annulment, abandonment, or when the grandparent's child is deceased. A grandparent may also petition when their child is the non-custodial parent and that parent has refused, failed or has been unable to have visitation for a period of 6 months or more or has been precluded from visitation with the child by court order or is in the Armed Services, stationed over 100 miles from the state border and the grandparent has been refused visitation with the child by the custodial parent for 6 months or more, also if a parent is deceased. Visitation is also permitted when the child has resided with the grandparent exclusively for 6 consecutive months within the previous 2 year period, the child was removed from the home by the parent, and the removing parent has refused visitation. Adoption terminates rights. 48-2B

WISCONSIN: Visitation is considered if the grandparent has maintained a close relationship with the child, the best interests and the wishes of the child, and if one of the parents is deceased. Adoption cuts off visitation unless by a stepparent. 880.155, 767.245

WYOMING: Visitation may be granted when the child of the grandparent is deceased and the custodial parent[person] has refused visitation, or if the parents of the child are divorced. Visitation may also be granted if the child resided with the grandparent for at least 6 months before returning to the custody of the parents and they have refused visitation with the child. The best interest of the child is considered and the court must find that the parents' rights are not impaired. Adoption terminates rights. 20-7-101

According to Judy Atkinson's article, "The Existence of Grandparent Rights Statutes in the United States" has effectively reduced the need for litigation[Wilson & DeShane,1982]." The fact that there is law reform designed to further rights of grandparents to see their grandchildren, is likely to act as a deterrent for the denied access and ultimately reduce the need for legal procedures. Atkinson continues, "Grandparents who found the threat of going to court effectively in resolving the denial of access certainly agreed that if a legislated the right to access was in place, then perhaps the adult–daughter-in-law would not have prevented access to begin with."

Conclusion

In conclusion, there are a few things that I would like to see happen. First, I would like to see national uniform grandparent rights laws. I would like to see the true best interest of the child considered, which means a mandated court appointed advocate for every child. Finally, simplify the criteria and eliminate specific conditions for the determination of the grandparent visitation rights to be granted. A grandparent is a grandparent and ignoring the strong bonds that exist between the grandparent and grandchild does not represent the best interests of the child. Why should it matter if the parents are married or not? Or one parent is deceased, or missing?

The grandparents play a significant role in the lives of children, it is a unique and separate relationship therefore, what is going on with the family should not determine the outcome of the relationship or pose a threat to the bond that has developed.

Chart 6: *Third-Party Visitation*

STATE	Stepparents	Grandparents—Death of their child	Grandparents—Child Divorce	Out of Wedlock	Any Interested Party
Alabama		x	x		
Alaska	x[4]	x	x	x	
Arizona	x[1]	x	x	x	
Arkansas		x	x		
California	x	x	x		
Colorado		x	x	x	
Connecticut	x	x	x	x	
Delaware	x		x		
District of Colombia					
Florida		x	x	x	
Georgia		x	x		
Hawaii	x		x		
Idaho			x	x	
Illinois	x	x		x	
Indiana	x	x	x	x	
Iowa					
Kansas	x	x	x	x	
Kentucky		x	x	x	
Louisiana		x	x		
Maine	x	x	x	x	
Maryland		x	x		
Massachusetts		x	x		
Michigan	x	x	x		
Minnesota	x	x	x	x	
Mississippi		x	x		
Missouri		x	x	x	
Montana		x	x	x	
Nebraska	x	x	x		
Nevada		x	x	x	
New Hampshire	x	x	x	x	
New Jersey	x	x	x	x	
New Mexico	x	x	x	x	
New York	x	x	x	x	
North Carolina			x		
North Dakota	x	x	x		
Ohio	x	x	x	x	x[2]
Oklahoma		x	x	x	
Oregon	x	x	x	x	
Pennsylvania		x	x		
Rhode Island		x	x		
South Carolina		x	x	x	
South Dakota		x	x	x	
Tennessee	x		x		
Texas	x	x	x	x	
Utah	x	x	x	x	
Vermont		x	x		
Virginia					x[3]
Washington	x		x		
West Virginia		x	x	x	
Wisconsin		x	x		
Wyoming	x	x	x		x

1. New in-loco-parentis bill allows visitation and in rare cases custody to these in loco parentis.
2. Extends only to relatives of minor child.
3. This includes any relative or a stepparent.
4. Only if stepparent is established as child's "psychological parent" under case law.

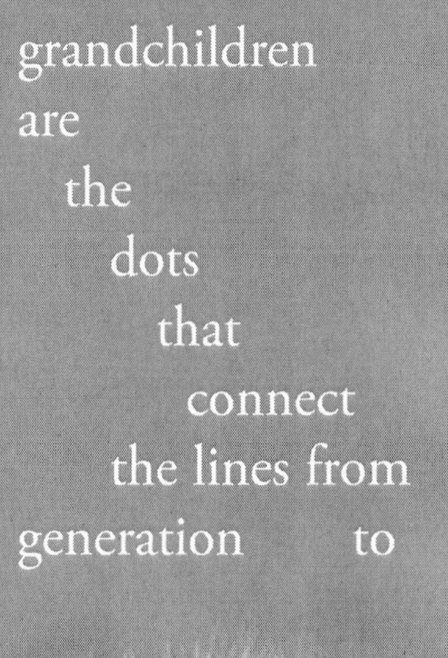

grandchildren
are
the
dots
that
connect
the lines from
generation to generation

-lois wyse

Eight

Grandparent Stories: Common Enemy Revealed

Cosmic Connection: The Tribe

I have lost consistent contact with my only grandson because the parents pulled up stakes and impulsively moved three thousand miles away. It was Thanksgiving and my son and daughter-in-law let it slip out that they were planning to move; I was devastated. I decided my mission would be to stop them by joining forces with the other biological grandmother of the half brother. My concern was that I would also be phased out like the other grandmother and lose visitation in the future.

My little grandson, and his older half brother have suddenly been isolated from their family, not to mention everything that they knew. The little one is in day care, when I could be watching him, and they both tell me how much they miss it here. There is a lack of family values an unstable and insecure situation, people have been cut off without conscious thouht. Grandparents offer a respite from dysfunctional families, as my own grandparents did, who happen to share the same first names as Susan's, hence, the 'Cosmic Connection.'

Grandparents gave me more of a feeling of a tribe. Grandma Jessie and grandpa Louie lived in Rialto and Riverside area and we went to their house to visit probably twice a month. My grandmother Jessie married my step-grandfather before I was born so he was always grandpa Louie. They were both great grandparents and I miss them to this day. Grandma was an Okie from the depression era and to support her children when she was single picked cotton in the Fresno area. Grandma was the glue that held the family together. She was a great cook and could make something from nothing. As soon as someone arrived at her house she would start cooking or we would get a root beer float. Everyone always felt welcome. She also could sew and apparently enjoyed it. She had six grand-daughters and every Christmas we would each get a hand made pair of pajamas and every Easter a new dress. She also made beautiful handmade quilts. I have 3 or 4 and have them repaired when they need it. I always have one on my bed. they will be handed down. Every holiday was spent with the whole family at her house or my aunts. My maternal grandmother, Esther, eventually moved to Huntington beach to be closer to us and we saw her all the time. I loved being with my grandparents and felt more secure knowing they were around. In honor of grandma Jessie, myself and my cousin named our children after her.

My aunt Virginia, Jessie's daughter and Marchelle's mom, lived in the immediate area, and after grandpa died, grandma Jessie came to live with her, even closer to me. I'm a hairdresser and every week I would drive to my aunt's and pick her up to do her hair and she would insist on making me lunch. You would never leave empty handed. She also would never let me do her hair for free. She stayed with my aunt for about 15 years until she died at 89.

Now that I'm a grandma I feel very deeply that I want to do the same for my grandchildren. Today only myself, my sister, my aunt and my cousin remain here. Everyone else has died or moved. I miss my tribe.

Grandma J. J.

Five Is Not Enough

We have not seen our two grandchildren in four years. It was my son and his wife who made that decision. He did not take his children into consideration when he decided upon this choice. He also alienated his sister and brother from his family. He grew up in a loving family which all of his friends admired and loved.

He cannot imagine the pain and heartache he has caused his family, cousins who were very close, to being estranged from, sister and brother who love him and who are shunned. Grandfather who thinks about his grandchildren at least 12 hours a day, he wonders what their thoughts and plans are, are they wondering why their extended family has no contact with them. A mother who would like to talk to her son and tell him how much she loves him, but he does not answer his phone or answer her letters.

I send cards to the children every month to say, "hello" and birthday cards on birthdays. I know they never receive them… I hope one day to tell them I never forgot them.

I am the fortunate one! I have four other grandchildren

and one on the way. I spend lots of time with them and enjoy all the moments of soccer, baseball and basketball, going to Disneyland, the beach and on vacations with our son and daughter and their families.

Our days are filled with these two wonderful children of ours and the sleepless nights are being replaced with the enjoyment we receive from the love and togetherness we have with our two children and grandchildren.

I hope and pray everyday that one day we will see our two grandchildren and my son.

I know in my heart my prayers will be answered.

These are my hopes and dreams.

Grandpa Earl, Grandma Linda

Eggshells

My daughter started to remove my husband and myself from her life after she married her second husband, even though it was me she called out for when she was approaching the delivery room with my second grandchild, my only granddaughter.

In the beginning we were very much a part of her new family, mostly because of my son-in-law. He wanted us to be a part of our granddaughter's life.

My daughter became more and more disrespectful, unloving and verbally abusive, not only with me, but with everyone around at different times. She has on occasion gotten physical with me, by pushing me, and once I saw her pull her husband's hair in anger. The abuse and distance became even worse after my grandson, who was at the time 18 years old, told her nicely but firmly at a ballet recital for my granddaughter, "mom, if you do not stop talking to grandma that way, I will leave."

Looking back, during my daughter's single years raising

Michael, there were times when she was close to me and times when she wasn't. My husband and I always made sure my daughter and my grandson had all the things they needed, including a home of their own. It was my gift so she and my grandson could live in a nice neighborhood.

A little over a year ago, I confronted my second daughter because she was inappropriately, in my mind, holding hands with my grandson's 18 year old friend. She did not seem affected by it and lovingly walked me to my car after the party. One week later she sent me the most hateful letter. I feel my other daughter stirred her up and things got out of hand, and now they are both angry. I wrote an apology letter and told her it was my problem.

Both my daughters seem to be full of anger and only remember the things they did not like about their childhood.

I have tried to call my granddaughter and my daughter always says she will call me back, even asking, "who is this?" I am extremely saddened not being able to see or talk to my granddaughter. What must she think? I want to be a part of my granddaughter's life. We are missing out on memories we cannot re-create.

I miss my granddaughter with all my heart and there is not a moment that goes by, I don't think of her. It has affected my life. I hear her everywhere I seem to be, at the grocery store, at the mall...I hear her calling..."Grandma", as I turn back to look and see her nowhere. I am a good and loving grandmother with a part of my heart missing. I think grandparents are extremely important, I can see that with my grandson.

Broken hearted grandmother

Where's Grandma?

My husband and I have lost visitation of our three grandchildren since June 2005, two years, now. It is because of a vicious daughter in law situation. They had a new baby recently, and never let us know. I have been in so much despair since this happened, but I have not given up, yet. The grandchildren are in an "intact" family.

If I give up, I will die of a broken heart. Please help me get this going in legislation. I have called my Assembly person's office and sent emails and nothing happened.

Not only am I a grandparent, I am a licensed therapist.

I am seeing the effects of families on grandkids cut off from their extended families because of family rifts and divorce or separation; the loss and grief of these children is tremendous. Their roots have been cut off. Their support and love have been instantly cut off. They have no rights and no control.

My youngest son, the grandkid's uncle shared with me that on a recent visit with them, he observed them pretending to call me on a cell phone, asking me to come visit. It is not the first time the children have demanded to see their grandma and insisted on spending the night.

I thought the kids would have forgotten us. I must fight for their rights; God given rights if anything even if the law of the land says that I can't.

Grandma Kay

Turned Tables

I lost my daughter, age 25 in July 2006. Her death was undetermined. She has 3 children, 8, 4 and 3. She never married the fathers, nor were they involved.

The father of the youngest children came to get them

with the police and a mysterious court order. Well, they took the 2 youngest babies. These children have lived with us since their births.

After the children were "legally kidnapped", they were taken to their grandparents in Missouri. They have been there since, and we have not seen them. They were ripped away from their only family and placed with total strangers. We have made attempts to contact, which have been unsuccessful; we are concerned about the safety of the children, given the father's past history.

We have gone to court in Illinois and the judge denied our petition. These children need us as we need them. Who will listen? Who do you go to? How do I find someone to listen? I need help, ideas, and whatever I can do. These were like my own children and this other family is hiding them from us. Why? It is like they are trying to get us to forget the kids and them us. They have however forgotten one thing, they left behind an 8 year old brother. He grieves for them everyday. He misses them so much and cries, what do I tell him? He doesn't understand. He said once, if he could just spend time with them and do things with them a few times a month, he would be happy.

It seems like the tables have turned to our benefit. Laws are very different in Missouri. The courts are more favorable towards us. The battle is not between the dad and us, now, it is between us and his father, the fraternal grandfather.

I have scheduled meetings with our state senator and state representative; I will meet with the governor if that's what it takes. These children should be with us, and we are just waiting for it to come.

Grandma Debra

Possession

Our son was killed in 2003 and until then we had a wonderful relationship with our grandchildren. But shortly after his death we were not allowed to see the children. In short, we have been trying to visit the children and have filed visitation petitions, but our daughter-in-law has moved several times and we have to keep changing jurisdictions to get a hearing. We were at one time, allowed to see to see them, but we never had a court order, just verbal agreement between attorneys.

I was always under the impression in Virginia that we had to prove it was in the best interest of the child to see us, and also prove that they would be harmed if they did not see us. Our attorney said that because of the Troxel case, there is very little hope for us to get visitation.

Our daughter-in-laws should realize these children are a gift to them, not a possession. One day they will be the grandmother also.

Grandmother D.

Two Weeks

Our three grandchildren [7,4,3] lived with us until October of 2006. Their mother, who had abandoned them about a year earlier, and married someone else, took them through the court.

Our son, the children's father is in prison right now, he and the children's mother were never married.

We just want to be a part of their lives. We tried going through the children's mother to see them and she let us see them one time in February. She told us we could see them again in two weeks at ten AM. When we went to see them we were met by her husband, and he said they were not there. We called and left messages and they won't return our calls.

When we saw our grandchildren back in February, they wanted to come home with us. It is hard not to see Lindsay, Robert and Daniel; it really hurts.

Grandma & Grandpa E.

Seashells

I have but just one grandchild, a boy, who is now 10 years old. It has been a year since I last saw him, and I remember every minute of our time together, especially that last day: Fathers Day June 18, 2006.

We were at the beach standing for hours collecting seashells. I was content just to hold the bucket while he dug for the treasures each time the tide carried in a new selection. Sometimes I would trap the shapeliest specimens under my feet, curling my toes deeply into the wet sand to resist losing them as the ocean pulled away; soon there would be an added surprise, once it was safe to lift my foot.

As I hugged him tightly and we each said, "I love you" as we said "goodbye"; somehow I knew it would be the last time for a long time.

Jacob's parents are embroiled in a custody battle, and as ridiculous as it is, my visitation with my grandson is an issue. The mother is set on controlling the child's life when she is not with him, therefore, the father's visitors to his home are not immune to the mother's scrutiny. The second part of her plan is to keep outside influences from others at a minimum by restricting visitation. Besides the possibility of counteracting mom's propaganda, I am a reminder of a past life, that she wants to have disappear. So much so, she is on a mission to convince the child that his adoptive father is his real father, hoping he will forget about the adoption procedure. Her preference is to live a lie.

Mom prevailed in the custody outcome. The adoptive dad acquiesced by submitting to her demands and threats and signed an agreement to keep me out of my grandson's life. No more cards, no gifts, no phone calls, no visits, when he is with either parent.

It seems like a selfish act for the parents to prevent a child from receiving love in the form of human contact and through symbolic well intended traditional gestures of kindness.

He is on my mind and in my heart every day; some days I grieve more than others. I miss him terribly and sadly he is missing out as well.

Once I happily settled for 60 seconds of hearing his voice in a speaker of a cell phone, with the help of a cooperative liason. At this point it is better than nothing.

Grandma Susan

Our grandchildren
accept us for ourselves, without
rebuke or effort to change us, as no
one in our entire lives has ever
done, not our parents, siblings,
spouses, friends-and hardly ever our
own grown children.

~ruth goode

Epilogue

Knowing where we came from is of vital importance to where we end up. We are influenced by what or who we have in our lives as well as what we don't have.

Simply knowing that there are others out there that share our heritage, our blood, our lineage provides security.

I once shared a bit of family history with Jacob as part of my ongoing journal-writing.

Dear Jacob,

Did you know that you are a link that created "FIVE" generations? That means without you there would not have been five generations. First there was great-great grandma, her son, then his daughter, me, then my son and daughter, and then my son's son, you! Upon your birth in 1997 and for the next five years until 2004 when great-great grandma Jessie died at 101 and 364 days(yes, the day before her

102nd birthday) we had five generations. Five generations is extremely rare; most families are comprised of three and not very often, four. It occurred to me that this was a significant occasion worth documenting.

It was December 4, 1999, you were an energetic two year old, and this would be the one and only time that you would meet your great-great grand-mother and she you. Mountains had to be moved to orchestrate the event. We received opposition from your mother, whose compliance occurred only as a result of an order from the court. There were no accommodations given us to extend the visitation time with a reasonable extension allowing for the extra driving distance to the retirement home. Somehow we pulled it off through a joint effort, getting everyone together for a once-in-a-lifetime photograph.

I remember every detail of that day and I feel grateful for the opportunity. It warms my heart that we were able to spend those few moments, frustration aside, with a whole and complete fully connected family. You were a perfect model that day, as you posed on command and showed off for the new audi-ence. Once all the photos were taken, you ran and played with a giant purple ball as all the adults looked on, occasionally snapping action shots. We now and forever have documented a small place in time and proof of a family that once was.

Everyone needs to have
access both to
grandparents
and
grandchildren in
order to be a
full human being.

~margaret mead

Resources

Divorce Poison by Richard Warshak, Ph. D., published by Regan Books, Harper-Collins, 2001.

The Essential Grandparent by Dr. Lillian Carson, Published by Health Communications, Inc., 1996.

The Essential Grandparent's Guide To Divorce by Lillian Carson, published by Health Communications, Inc., 1999.

Grandparents' Rights by Patricia Slorah, P.h. D., published by Patricia Slorah, 2003.

The Grandparent Guide by Arthur Kornhaber, M.D., published by Contemporary Books, McGraw-Hill Co., 2002.

Grandparent Organizations:

AARP

www. aarp.org
Aarp Foundation Grandparent Information Center
601 E. St. NW
Washington, DC 20049
888-687-2277

Advocates For Grandparent-Grandchild Connection

www.grandparentchildconnect.org
PO BOX 5622
Newport Beach, California, 92662
949-640-0399

Cangrands

www.cangrands.com
Ontario Canada
613-474-0035

Grandparents-R-Us

www.grandparents-r-us.com
PO BOX 418
Patton, California 92369
909-885-1324

THE FOUNDATION FOR GRANDPARENTING

www.grandparenting.org

THE NATIONAL COMMITTEE OF GRANDPARENTS FOR CHILDREN'S RIGHTS

www.grandparentsforchildren.org
PO BOX 6635
Albany, New York 12206
866-624-9900

Susan is a true advocate who saw a flaw in the system that emotionally harms children and is working to change that.

She is also the best kind of advocate — she speaks from the heart.

Brigitte Castellano
Executive Director
National Committee of Grandparents for Children's Rights
www.grandparentsforchildren.org
866-624-9900